Conversations with Mom:

Recipes for Self-Help

Amani Dusi, PhD

To My Extraordinary Mother,

Conversations with you never fail to amaze me; they completely captivate my mind and soul. The wisdom you impart is like a magical dance where all the pieces come together in perfect harmony, filling my universe with love and tranquility. I am grateful for every conversation we've had, and I eagerly look forward to the countless more we will share. Thank you for being such an amazing presence in my life.

To my greatest treasures, Elena and Nadine. This is for you.

About the Author

Step into Amani Dusi's world, where the warmth of California's sun embraces the aroma of freshly baked goods. With a doctorate in leadership for the advancement of learning and service, she blends academic prowess with a unique life perspective. Living with her loving, supportive husband and two adorable daughters – aged 2 and 4 – her life is a symphony of love and laughter. Amani's one-hand writing style, while cradling a baby in the other, is a testament to her dedication to her writing.

INTRODUCTION

People's reactions when they meet my mother are always filled with curiosity and amazement. They often find themselves asking, "Who are you?" and "What are you?" Her presence and interactions defy easy categorization, as if she carries an aura of light and openness that draws people in. She can have meaningful conversations with individuals from all walks of life, regardless of language or background. She possesses an incredible gift for forming connections.

I didn't always have a strong relationship with my mom. I began to truly appreciate her when I started understanding her and applying her advice, witnessing the results of her wisdom in my own life. Along with my siblings, we grew up in a very conservative culture where I wasn't allowed to do many things that boys could do. Despite this, my mom somehow instilled in my sister and me a sense of strength and power that still makes us feel capable of conquering the world.

I used to wish my mom would be more obedient to social norms. It was around the time when I was 12 years old, after a mothers' meeting at my all-girls school, that my mom did something incredibly brave. She confronted the most intimidating teacher there and insisted she be kind to us girls, treat us gently, and show us respect. In that moment, all the heads of my classmates turned around and stared at me with wide eyes. The girls couldn't believe that someone dared to confront this teacher. I felt a strong desire for the ground to open up and swallow me.

When I got home, I told Mom she should be like the other moms. She asked what I meant, and I simply said, "Just be like them." Then, she suddenly told me to go to my room and asked if I'd done my homework. I admitted I hadn't, and she said I wasn't behaving. I was angry and confused. I looked at her and said, "What's happening?" Her response surprised me, "This is me trying to be like the other moms." I didn't like that, so I told her to go back to being herself, my mom. Eventually, she agreed and said, "Ok, now I am back to being your mom. Let's talk about these feelings and figure out where they came from and how to remove them and move on."

Mom always stood out with her blonde hair, fair skin, and bubbly personality. Sometimes I thought she was too much for the environment she was in; everyone always stared at her, even in an all-girls school. She never quite fit in, and I didn't truly appreciate that at the time.

She let me play with anything that was safe to play with as a child; I used to enjoy borrowing her makeup and high heels, while my cousins who were my age could only dream of trying them on. They often came over to my house to play.

Now, looking back, I appreciate that she allowed me to feed my curiosity.

I began to truly listen to my mom when I was at my lowest point, striving hard to achieve my adult dreams. She pushed me to achieve them, being there every step of the way with her wisdom on how to maintain a healthy mind and soul. I was able to achieve all my dreams, thanks in large part to her unwavering support. Her insight and wisdom weren't innate; she gained them over the years through learning, meditation, silence, and hard work.

After all of us, her five kids, moved out of the house, she embarked on a new chapter, moving to a beach house on the Mediterranean Sea, in a country where she initially knew no one. She spent the first two years there, taking walks on the beach, and watching the daily sunsets and sunrises. She referred to this time as a period of emotional cleansing, thought decluttering, and soul-healing. My mom is a remarkable woman, and her strength lies in her relationship and dedication to God.

Now, Mom still lives in her beach house on the Mediterranean Sea, surrounded by friends. Everyone knows her in the neighborhood because, at some point, when they needed advice, Mom was there to give it to them. The pharmacist, the grocer, the baker, the hairdresser—they all look for her. Mom thinks of this as a gift from God; she possesses the ability to talk to people, and after just one conversation, they feel relief.

Most of the conversations in this book happen in person when she takes a few months off from her life, traveling overseas, to join mine. During her visits, she helps me with anything I need from doing laundry, to caring for my emotional health through these meaningful chats. The moment my mom enters my house, I feel relieved, as if I can take a vacation from the stress of life. When she isn't visiting, we talk on the phone every day, or I ask her a question and she responds in a voice recording if she's not available when I call.

INTRODUCTION

From her advice, I have seen significant results and relief that have led me to truly accomplish all my dreams. I decided I wanted to write our conversations down; I did not want to forget them, and I wanted my kids to read them and learn from them one day. As I started recording them, I realized these conversations had to be available for others to read also.

These conversations with Mom are delicious morsels of wisdom, packed with information that blows the mind away. While each exchange may only span a page or two, their impact is immeasurable. After delving into these conversations, I often find myself seeking a quiet place to sit and truly absorb their significance. It's like unpacking a treasure trove, analyzing every word, and meditating on the profound facts they hold. They become valuable tools in my emotional toolbox, ready to be applied whenever I need them.

This isn't just a quick read; it's a reference, a book to be studied and revisited. It's a journey of perspectives. I learn, then go back, read again, and soak up the wisdom. Whenever I find myself in a new situation where I need guidance, I return once more. Each reading unveils new layers of insight.

Contents

Contents

The Rocket Of Life: Prepare For Your Blast Off

Outside was gloomy like the start of a storm may be brewing in the distance, but inside was warm and cozy, like being wrapped in a soft blanket. The smell of cinnamon spice floated on the steam from the tea kettle and wafted into my nose. I took a big inhale savoring the calming aroma. Mom sat on our blue couch with a comforting cup of tea in hand, her gaze serious and inquisitive. "Describe to me, what is life?" she asked, prompting a moment of self-reflection.

I felt a twinge of nervousness, the same unease as if I were back in school facing an examination. "I feel like I'm being put to the test. Some people believe life encompasses everything, but..."

Mom interrupted and said, "I want to know your perspective, not what others think. Tell me your explanation of life."

Taking a moment to gather my thoughts, I responded, "Well, I see life as a grand opportunity—a precious gift with a limited timeframe, maybe a hundred years if we're fortunate, to shape our destinies in any way we desire. It's akin to having a piece of dough placed in our hands; with that simple dough, I can transform it into various wonders—a loaf of bread, a delightful waffle with butter, eggs, and sugar, or even a delectable cake by adding moisture and milk. Life, too, presents us with a myriad of elements, and it's our creative spirit that guides us in how we utilize them—creating something truly unique or leaving them untouched to dry and eventually be discarded."

Then my Mom asked, "But what is your view of life when you're depressed? How would you describe it then?"

Reflecting on those dark days of postpartum depression, I vividly recalled feeling life was a heavy burden, an overwhelming load to bear. "I thought of life as something burdening me, a curse laid upon my shoulders," I answered honestly.

My mom responded, "Life remains the same whether you're mentally in a good place or a difficult one. What truly changes is your perspective, which consequently changes your experience of life as well.

"I understand what it's like to be in those low places. I, too, have had days when life felt burdensome. However, if I hadn't experienced those moments, I wouldn't have delved into searching for meaning and raising my awareness. Sometimes, those dark days are gifts that prompt us to explore the purpose of our lives and seek out opportunities.

"Life is like a rocket. You need the sparks, the ignition, and the fire to build until finally, the explosion propels the rocket through the nozzle. Those explosions are similar to the hardships we face while still in one place, serving as catalysts for us to discover our true calling in the universe. Not everyone is a rocket, but many people endure difficulties and eventually recover, launching themselves toward their destined accomplishments.

"In this book, we aim to assist those who are in the burning stage of life, just before the moment they blast off.

"Maintain a positive outlook on your own life, and when those tough days come, consider them as sparks necessary to propel your rocket toward the universe."

66

Maintain a positive outlook on your own life, and when those tough days come, consider them as sparks necessary to propel your rocket toward the universe.

99

Protect Your Diamond: Nurturing Your Dreams In Silence

I found Mom sitting serenely in her room, engrossed in her well-worn prayer book—a testament to years of faithful use. Knocking gently on the door, I asked, "May I come in?" With a warm smile, she welcomed me, inviting me to share in her world for a moment. As I settled in, she shared a captivating Arabic phrase that held great significance upon reflection.

"Daro omorakom be al kitman," which means, "Manage your affairs in silence." This saying holds a profound meaning; suggesting that when you embark on something significant, keep your intentions to yourself until you've accomplished your goal.

I pondered whether sharing my goals could aid me in achieving them. Almost as if she could hear my thoughts, Mom replied,

"It's not just about the plans you make; it's about the intentions you hold behind those plans."

She illustrated the difference between someone who openly expresses their desire to buy a house and involves family and friends in the process, versus someone who quietly acquires the house before revealing the purchase.

"Imagine your intention as a radiant diamond," Mom said. "When a single beam of light shines upon the stone, a beautiful rainbow emerges on the other side. The light represents your desired energy, while the diamond symbolizes your intention.

"However, if you disclose your plans to others, you invite a multitude of opinions and comments. These various perspectives act as multiple lights shining on your diamond, causing it to lose its brilliance and hide the rainbow. Keep your grand dreams, desires, and intentions within, while letting go of negative emotions."

"Confide in your dreams and hopes," she continued, "for whatever you hold in your heart will grow with you. But if unwelcome feelings arise, release them, and let them go. It is a secret from the universe's wisdom to approach your endeavors with serenity, and to keep your aspirations confidential."

After Mom finished her coffee, she stood and declared, "Now, let's get ready to head to the beach."

Little did I know that this ordinary moment would soon become extraordinary, this secret held the power of transformation – my perspective was changed.

As I sit now in my beautiful garden, surrounded by the tranquility of my new home, I reflect on that profound conversation and its impact on my journey. By protecting the radiance of my "diamond," my dreams and ambitions, I fulfilled my heart's desires.

"

It's not just about the plans you make; it's about the **intentions** you hold behind those plans.

"

Love Beyond Distance: Letting Go Of Egos and Expectations

was once deeply in love with a man who lived far away, and I found myself in a painful long-distance relationship. One day in particular, I opened my computer with a great sadness, waiting for my boyfriend to come online and chat with me. I longed for a hug, a touch, and to feel his presence. I wondered how much longer I could endure this distance. What would happen to us? Was he meant to be my future husband? If so, why wasn't he here?

I contemplated breaking up with him. I couldn't see the relationship progressing beyond the confines of the screen. "Mom," I said, feeling stuck, "I've been in a long-distance relationship for four years, and it doesn't seem to be going anywhere. He's involved in his work and life there; I'm busy with projects, university, and life here. It hurts. What should I do?"

She brought a pot of fragrant mint tea, infused with delicate pink flower petals. It was a traditional mint and flower tea, a signature brew from the place where she grew up. Pouring a cup for herself and one for me, she settled beside me, her presence comforting and reassuring. With a sip of the soothing tea, I listened as she responded to my concerns.

"The problem is that you've invested all your emotions and thoughts into this one relationship. It's time to let go of these attachments. Sometimes, it's a small fear, the natural fear that arises when embarking on something new. Other times, it's a deeper and more complex fear that paralyzes us from taking any action.

"Self-destruction begins when our feelings don't align with our desires. Right now, you're feeling afraid and maybe even unworthy of this relationship, but your desire is to be with this person. This conflict within you is causing self-destruction.

"True improvements in your life and situation will occur only when your feelings and desires are in harmony. I want you to always strive for this inner peace and harmony. Don't let self-destruction take over.

"What you can do right now is change your feelings to align with your thoughts. Your relationship is within your control, in your hands only. Close your eyes and imagine the feeling of safety and happiness with your husband in your home. Picture him holding you and experience the security and joy you've never felt before. Desire the long-term, blissful marriage you envision. Don't let your ego interfere with these feelings and desires. Love wholeheartedly and unconditionally."

"But how can I do that?" I asked.

"Love that involves thoughts of losing or gaining is conditional love," Mom said. "Love isn't about winning or losing. What you're doing now is loving with expectations of having him here and now. Love without ego. When I told you to be with someone who will give you a life, I meant don't marry someone who will confine you to their world or prevent you from being who you truly are.

"Otherwise, you'll end up feeling alone. Marry someone who allows you the freedom to live your life to the fullest, without limits; just like what you have now. When I talk about loving without ego, it's like the way I love you. I don't expect anything in return except for your happiness, peace, and love. When a mother loves with ego, she expects things like her daughter's time and care in return.

"Reset your love for him. Love him unconditionally, but don't invest all your emotions solely in this relationship. It isn't your entire world. You have your studies, family, dreams, and accomplishments. He is just one part of your big, beautiful heart. Love him boundlessly, and before you know it, he will be by your side as your husband."

As I write this, sitting by my husband's side in a coffee shop, enjoying coffee and a chocolate croissant, I reflect on this conversation thirteen years ago. That long-distance boyfriend I contemplated ending things with is now my loving husband and father of our two beautiful girls. Today we're discussing which painting to hang in our new home that we recently purchased together, and I'm so thankful I could learn to love him without ego or expectation.

"

Self-destruction begins when our feelings don't align with our desires

"

Understanding Ego: Navigating Insecurity

As mom and I prepared a mouthwatering dish called Shrimp Biryani, the aromatic spices filled the kitchen, the tantalizing scent intermingled with our conversation. Shrimp, tender and succulent, mingled with fragrant Basmati rice, each grain perfectly cooked. We blended a combination of spices, infusing the dish with a symphony of flavors that danced on our taste buds.

While the biryani simmered to perfection, we decided to serve it with a side of plain yogurt, its cool creaminess providing a delightful contrast to the bold spices of the main dish. We garnished the yogurt with fresh mint, cilantro, and crisp cucumber slices, creating a yogurt salad that would refresh the palate between bites of the flavorful shrimp biryani.

After we finished cooking, I turned my attention to the toys that littered my children's room. It felt like a giant sigh escaped my lips every time I looked around at the mess. I have always been someone who appreciates a neat and organized space, but having little ones has taught me a lot about the challenges of maintaining a tidy house.

I moved around the room with determination, diligently picking up toys and making an effort to clear the clutter in order to create a more organized and inviting space. The physical effort took a toll on my back, and I could feel it beginning to ache from all the bending and lifting. Needing a moment of respite, I decided to sit down for a while, and my mom, ever the helpful presence, joined me, folding laundry with her characteristic calmness.

In her reassuring company, I felt comfortable and decided to share my experiences of the day.

"I came across some people today who seemed to have really big egos. It was hard to deal with them," I said.

"Ah, yes," Mom responded. "Encountering individuals with inflated egos can be challenging. How did you handle it?"

"I didn't really know what to do," I replied. "It felt like they thought they were superior to everyone else, always trying to control and advise others."

"I understand," Mom said. "When someone displays a big ego, it often comes from a place of thinking they are better or more successful than others. They may try to interfere in people's lives, believing they know what's best for them."

"That's exactly how they acted!" I said. "How can I deal with such people?

"One approach is to focus on their good qualities," Mom replied. "Try to step into their shoes and understand their struggles and insecurities. For example, consider how they might feel the need to keep their child safe or constantly prove their parenting skills."

"That makes sense. So, their defensiveness is actually rooted in insecurity?" I asked.

"Yes, exactly," Mom said. "Insecure individuals often become defensive. Similarly, when our own egos start showing up, it's because we feel undeserving of something. It could be positive or negative, but that feeling of not deserving is the same. When you notice your ego surfacing, take a moment to reflect on yourself."

"What about when someone hurts us? Is that connected to ego too?" I wondered.

"Absolutely, feeling hurt by someone is often tied to our ego. When we allow ourselves to be hurt by others, it indicates a lack of harmony within ourselves. When we are truly aligned with our inner selves, people who want to hurt us won't even cross our path."

"That's interesting. Ego can vary in intensity among individuals?"

"Yes, dear, some people have a larger portion of ego, while others have less. Ego tends to manifest through possessiveness, especially in relationships like marriage or between parents and children. When we try to control our loved ones' behaviors and view their actions as a reflection of our own success, that's our ego at play."

"I never realized that before. And ego can manifest in different ways too?"

"Absolutely," Mom said. "Pay attention to how people react around you. If someone says they don't want to be with you or rejects a gift, and you feel hurt or think you don't deserve their response, that's your ego reacting."

"Wow, this knowledge is eye-opening."

"It's always important to navigate ego with empathy and self-reflection," Mom said as she continued calmly folding the laundry.

Understanding Ego

"

When we allow ourselves
to be hurt by others,
it indicates a lack
of **harmony** within
ourselves.

"

Embracing The Joys Of Motherhood: Grab A Spoon And Dig In

Being a mom to an active and curious two-year-old is an exhausting experience. My little one is always on the move, often getting into risky situations like climbing a teetering tower of blocks trying to reach my hot coffee mug on the ledge of the counter. It feels like my heart is in my throat all the time, and I struggle to get a good night's sleep because she wakes up frequently always needing the comfort of my touch. After one such exhausting night, I reached a breaking point and decided to call Mom to express my overwhelming feelings about the immense difficulties of motherhood.

I confided in my mom, telling her that everyone advises me to cherish every moment because time flies and children grow up quickly. They urge me to appreciate the beauty of these early years. However, I find it challenging to enjoy this time, amidst the pressures and demands of being a mother. Sometimes the beauty of childhood is clouded with never-ending laundry, dishes in the sink, toys all over the floor, and an exhaustion that feels all-consuming. At times I find myself wondering, "How can I possibly find joy in this situation?"

Mom offered me some wise words: "It all boils down to expectations. Instead of setting high expectations for everything, take life as it comes. If something happens, let it happen. If you wake up in the middle of the night or if you struggle to accomplish tasks due to constant interruptions, accept it as part of the journey. Even if you have to eat your lunch standing or miss a meal, it's okay. Life is full of obstacles, but if you learn to see them as gifts, you can find peace and harmony.

"Do not treat life like a rigid equation – 1+1=2 – with strict rules and expectations. Life is boundless and unpredictable. Instead of imposing definitions and labels on it, we should experience it as it is. The past is behind us, and the future is beyond our control. If we constantly plan every second, we end up living in the future, missing out on the sweetness of the present moment."

Mom suggested a simple exercise: "Look in the mirror when thinking about the future and see the joy in your eyes when truly living in the moment. Living in the present is like savoring a bowl of salted caramel ice cream. As you indulge in each spoonful, fully immersed in the experience, you taste the coldness melting in your mouth, relish the smooth texture, and embrace the occasional burst of saltiness. Every bite brings the delightful unpredictability of caramel sauce, making each moment unique."

Living in the moment enhances the pleasure of life. Whatever we do, it should bring us joy. Even the simplest tasks can be enjoyable when approached with presence and mindfulness. Now as I navigate the joys and challenges of motherhood, I remind myself to let go of rigid expectations, embrace the uncertainty of life, and find pleasure in every experience. The equations of life may not have fixed answers, but by living fully, we can grab that bowl of salted caramel ice cream and relish each delicious spoonful.

"

Life is full of **obstacles**, but if you learn to see them as gifts, you can find peace and harmony.

"

Lifelong Friendship: Finding Fun In Every Moment

When I was in graduate school, I was filled with insecurity and worry, wondering if I could endure the challenges of the program. Little did I know that a chance encounter would change my entire experience, leading to a lifelong friendship.

It all began on the first day of orientation when I met a remarkable woman who would soon become my best friend. Amidst a room full of strangers, she approached me with familiarity and warmth. To my surprise, she turned out to be the international student adviser, defying my preconceived notions of her appearance. Her youthful energy and colorful attire made me feel instantly at ease.

From that moment on, she became an integral part of my life, accompanying me through major milestones. She stood by me as I completed my MBA, my Ph.D., officiated my wedding, witnessed the births of my children, and offered unwavering support during both triumphs and heartbreaks. Her friendship has been a blessing, and I cherish her dearly.

I was reflecting on this special friendship with Mom, and I shared a valuable lesson I learned from my friend about careers. She had a simple yet profound rule: If work stops being fun, it's time to move on to new opportunities. I recounted an incident when she came to my house one day from work, utterly exhausted. She laid down on my couch and asked to borrow my computer.

Determined to lift her spirits, I gave her the laptop and went to the kitchen to prepare a quick dessert I often made - "moon flakes," a variation of crispy treats made with cornflakes and marshmallows. I hoped this sweet treat would help her forget about her tough day. When I returned to the living room, I noticed a change had come over her while I was out of the room. She looked relieved, and her eyes sparkled with newfound enthusiasm. She closed the borrowed computer and revealed that she was quitting her job the next day. Moreover, she had applied for a job in Boston. I was astounded, nearly dropping the moon flakes in shock.

In a matter of weeks, she secured the job, relocated to Boston, and embarked on a career she loved. There, she found not only professional fulfillment but also the love of her life, the man who later became her husband.

After listening intently to the story that I recounted, my mom shared her wisdom: "There are only a few people who know how to be happy, and that is their default mode." She emphasized the importance of pleasure and happiness, explaining, "Pleasure is the driving force that brings love, happiness, and meaning to our lives. It is essential to define what brings us joy and incorporate pleasurable moments into our daily routines, especially when something feels missing.

"Find fun even in tasks you don't particularly enjoy. Whether it's going to a dreaded dentist appointment or cleaning the house, use your imagination to transport yourself to exciting places. Everything can be turned into an opportunity for fun."

In that moment, Mom and I decided to indulge in a delicious treat – a homemade vanilla pound cake, with the addition of dark chocolate chips to make it extra special. As we ate each bite, we realized that life's journey should be filled with pleasure and enjoyment, seeking out experiences that bring us joy and fulfillment.

And so, armed with my friend's valuable lesson and Mom's wise words, I embarked on a mission to embrace fun, pleasure, and happiness in all aspects of my life.

"

Find fun even in tasks you don't enjoy. Whether it's going to a dreaded dentist appointment or cleaning the house, use your imagination to transport yourself to exciting places. Everything can be turned into an opportunity for fun.

"

Baking From The Heart: Infusing Love Into All You Do

"Oh, the aroma of a freshly baked pound cake always brings such tranquility to the kitchen," Mom said. "I love seeing you bake, dear. It's like watching you meditate."

The warm scent of vanilla and sugar filled the kitchen and gave the whole room an aroma that calmed the senses. Flour and baking powder speckled the counter, but the mess didn't overwhelm me, not while I was in my happy place.

"Thank you, Mom," I said. "Baking truly does make me feel centered and accomplished. There's something magical about creating something delicious from scratch. It's a form of self-expression."

"Make love the heart of everything you do," Mom responded. "Just like that cake you're making right now. You're pouring love into each step, and the result will be amazing—a moist and flavorful cake that will bring joy to everyone who tastes it."

"How do we infuse love into everything we do, Mom?" I asked. "It sounds wonderful, but I want to understand how to truly embody it."

"Start by filling yourself with love," Mom said. "Love yourself first and foremost. The more you love yourself, the more love you'll have to give. And when you give love freely, you'll receive even more in return. It's one of the secrets of the universe."

"That's profound, Mom. So, where does this love come from?" I inquired.

"The source of love is divine, it comes from God—from the universe," she replied. "We need to connect with that source, tap into its pure love. Each person has their own way of doing that. Some find it through fasting, some through meditation or yoga, some through prayer, and others by admiring the beauty of nature. Find your way to replenish that love within you from the source itself."

"I understand now," I said. "Once we know our source of love, we need to make sure we visit it often to keep our love tank full."

"Exactly, my dear. And when you infuse everything you do with that love—whether it's baking a cake or any other task—you'll notice the difference. Love adds a special touch, a certain magic that transforms the ordinary into the extraordinary," Mom concluded.

The timer dinged and I pulled the cake from the oven. Instantly the tantalizing scent filled the kitchen.

"Look, Mom, it looks perfect!" I exclaimed. "Let's put it on the cooling rack and resist the temptation to slice it right away."

"Oh, that's going to be hard, but we know that good things come to those who wait," Mom answered.

A few moments later, unable to resist any longer, I grabbed a knife and sliced into the still-warm cake.

"Here you go, Mom. A slice of love-filled deliciousness, just for you," I said.

We laughed as we blew on our slices, savoring the warmth and love that radiated from the cake. Mom pronounced the flavor amazing, adding, "Even though it's hot, the love you put into making this cake shines through in every bite."

"

Love yourself first and foremost. The more you love yourself, the more love you will have to give.

"

The Sun And Clouds: Understanding Reality And Illusion

The day began with freshly brewed coffee and the sweet anticipation of my favorite breakfast—tahini with a delightful drizzle of date syrup. My mother toasted the whole wheat pita bread halves, giving them a delightful crunch. Each bite reminded me of the warmth of home. While pouring tea from the French press, my mom had a realization.

"Do you know the difference between illusion and reality?" she asked. I thought for a second and replied, "illusion is when you imagine things that aren't real. Reality is what's actually true."

Mom smiled and nodded. "Exactly. But now I understand reality and illusion even better. Let me explain. Illusion happens when we imagine the worst things and feel scared or uncertain about new experiences or the future.

"Reality is about life, death, new beginnings, and marriage. But illusion is the fear that covers up these real things. It's like the sun—always there, but sometimes clouds come and block it. The clouds are like scary thoughts that hide the sun of reality. The truth is always about love, peace, and joy. Illusion is just the negative thoughts that bring us down."

I listened, trying to grasp her words. "But Mom," I said, "sometimes there are genuinely scary things. Shouldn't we be afraid of them?"

Mom gently held my hand and reassured me, "there's nothing inherently

scary, my dear. We make things scarier by thinking and imagining more. When we're scared or have disturbing thoughts, we need to focus on what's real and let go of uncertainty."

We enjoyed our breakfast together, savoring the moment. Mom kindly offered me more coffee, breaking the silence. I accepted with gratitude, appreciating the simple act of being together.

In our conversation, I learned that reality and illusion are like a dance. The sun of truth always shines, but the clouds of illusion come and go based on our thoughts and emotions. By embracing the present moment and letting go of negative thoughts, we find comfort in the radiant reality—where love, peace, and joy reside.

The Sun And Clouds

"

We make things scarier by thinking and imagining more. When we're scared or have disturbing thoughts, we need to **focus** on what's real and let go of uncertainty.

"

Discovering True Joy: Moving Beyond Illusions and enjoying Hessa

Mom and I decided to recreate my grandmother's treasured recipe: Hessa. It was a simple yet delicious combination of dates, whole wheat flour, ghee, cooked together in a pan, spiced with cinnamon, ginger, and cardamom, finally topped with roasted sesame seeds for that perfect finishing touch. The aroma of this treat filled the kitchen with the welcoming fragrance of dates caramelizing with butter, releasing their sweet and slightly nutty flavors.

With each passing moment, the scent of Hessa grew richer, like a symphony of flavors in the making. It was as if the kitchen itself had come to life, telling stories of generations past through its aromatic embrace.

Alongside Hessa, we brought a pot of aromatic Arabian coffee. This coffee was made from lighter roasted coffee beans infused with cardamom spice, lovingly boiled in water to create a fragrant brew. We carried Hessa, the coffee pot, and a set of small mugs to the cozy corner of our home. There, we poured the fragrant coffee and settled down to tackle the mountain of laundry that awaited us.

The pile seemed endless, and I couldn't help but think, "Wasn't I just doing laundry yesterday?" The never-ending cycle of clothes being washed, folded, and worn again felt like a constant in my life. How much more laundry would end up strewn about the floor of my children's room today?

Frustration bubbling up, I mentioned aloud how this chore seemed to have no end in sight. It was then that Mom offered a different perspective, suggesting that we fold the laundry together. She shared a valuable insight, saying that if I kept believing the laundry would never end, it never would.

Curious, I asked Mom to explain why people often bring on their own suffering. She said our thoughts, emotions, and beliefs about others can create negativity.

"When we compare ourselves or obsess over what people do, we end up in a bad place," Mom continued. "There's a saying in Arabic that describes the problem: 'observing people leads to burdens.'"

Mom persisted, saying that even small things, like hearing bad news about someone we know, can make us fear for our own safety. "Most of our suffering comes from others—someone stealing from us, having a better life, or causing problems," she said, "but here's the secret: there are no others, there are just our own reflections on others."

Amused, Mom said it's about connecting to something bigger than individuals. She explained that what we see as people are only reflections of our thoughts and emotions. To disconnect from suffering caused by others, we need to connect with a higher source.

Curious about how to disconnect, I asked Mom for advice. She said, "the shift starts by being aware of how we fill our minds with trivial details, like someone being rude or dishonest. Focusing on these things distracts us from the bigger picture." Mom emphasized that love is the key to true joy and connection.

To illustrate, Mom used coffee as an example. "Drinking the beverage only for caffeine won't bring enjoyment and might harm us," she said. "But when we drink coffee out of love and enjoyment, the drink becomes beneficial and pleasurable. Similarly, when we approach life with love, connection, and peace, nothing from the outside can harm us. Remember, there are no people—only reflections of our thoughts and emotions on people."

Mom's wisdom showed me that suffering caused by others is an illusion. By disconnecting from negativity and embracing love, joy, and peace, we rise above the influence of others. It's all about nurturing our inner world. So, let's discover true joy by loving beyond the realm of others.

> Most of our sufering
> comes from others,
> but here's the secret:
> there are no others,
> there are just our own
> **reflections** on others.

Expectations and the Art of Optimism

Mom and were prepared to cook one of our favorite dishes – my grandfather's recipe, "Kebab Sabanak," meaning spinach kebab. It's a simple recipe, and every time I indulge, it feels like my grandfather is giving me a hug. My mother's father was a cook, and cooking was his passion. He could spend hours in the kitchen, cooking and inventing recipes. Mom, however, disliked his cooking because she always had to help and be his sous chef. When he cooked, it went on for days, with everyone assigned a task. Mom often found herself spending hours in the kitchen with dough – filling it, rolling it, cutting it. I believe this has created a core memory for her, leading her to stop eating anything doughy to this day. My grandfather's grandparents came from Turkey, and his grandfather was a baker. He came on a pilgrimage to the holy mosque with his wife and child. They decided to stay in the holy land, finding opportunities to bake something different from what the locals were used to. This was a time and hub for trading goods and services when people from all around the world came together, bringing their cultures and goods during the pilgrimage.

My grandfather learned from his parents and grandparents to cook the Ottoman Empire's food, which they brought from Turkey. He eventually became the cook for the king. One amusing family story recounts the king's request for the "shaky desert," meaning pudding. At the time, the king of the holy land couldn't pay my grandfather in money. Instead, he compensated him with lands and citizenship as he worked on unifying the Arabian Peninsula. Later, when the country was established, my grandfather became one of the richest men in his town.

The spinach kebab was one of my mom's favorite recipes to make and share because it didn't require much time in the kitchen. Mom always says there are so many recipes we can make in minutes; we just need to learn them and master them. We prepared this dish by first gathering the ingredients, In a bowl, we added ground beef, spinach, dill, cilantro, basmati rice, onion, and garlic, mixing them well with a gloved hand. In a large pot that isn't too deep and has a cover, we greased it with ghee and created meatball-like shapes, placing them one by one in the pot. We added tomato paste and water until it covered the meatballs up to an inch. We covered the pot, placed it on the stove at low heat, and cooked it slowly for about 35 to 45 minutes until the rice and meat were cooked. The aroma of the kebab filled the air, reminiscent of a proper healthy meal from our grandparents' kitchen. Mom served the kebab with a white rice and green side salad.

While eating, I asked Mom if this was exactly what I had in mind for today. I didn't know what I wanted to eat, but I knew I wanted to feel like this. Then, I thought if I had anything else today, I would be disappointed. So, I asked Mom, "By the way, do we get disappointed? And how do we avoid disappointment?"

Mom said, "We get disappointed because we have expectations. We should replace expectations with positive experiences. Expecting something from others can often end in disappointment. Instead of expecting, replace it with optimism. You weren't expecting to have this exact dish today, but you were optimistic that Mom would cook something healthy and delicious for you today.

You can be optimistic about people's behaviors, be optimistic about what you will gain from a meeting with someone, for example, instead of expecting. Be optimistic that people around you are loyal and will serve you well. Be optimistic, for example, that the vaccine will give you immunity and make you stronger, that your body is healthy and won't catch that virus. Be optimistic that your relationships will grow and blossom. There is a difference between expectations and optimism. Expectations will leave you disappointed when you don't get exactly what you thought you would get; however, optimism can improve your outlook on life.

I asked, "But Mom, how do we not expect? This is hard. We expect certain behaviors from people; we expect to get the things we worked hard for. We certainly expect that my partner will get me something nice on Valentine's Day." Mom said, "Well, here comes the diligent practice. It's like anything in life – to be good at it, you need to put it into practice."

While I was eating the kebab, I said, "Mom, this is out of this world. It's so good; it really feels like a hug. Thank you." Mom said, "Just like this kebab we just made, it took me years to perfect my father's recipe. I think I make it better than he does now," she laughed.

Mom continued, "Remember that time when you wanted to learn how to make that perfect Liege waffle? How many batches of waffles did you make until you reached the perfect batch? Or learned that the secret ingredient all along was in one single ingredient – the pearl sugar that would caramelize the waffle iron, creating a crispy exterior with a chewy interior.

Replacing the expectation with optimism will require you to have diligent practice within every situation. Until you find your pearl sugar of happiness, keep practicing."

Lessons In A Tea Shop: Letting Go Of Loss

Mom and I talk almost every day, even though there's a ten-hour time difference between us. If we can't talk during my day or her night, she sends me a recording with answers to my questions or updates.

Recently, Mom sent me a recording apologizing for not being able to talk. She went to the movies and lost track of time.

I replied with a recording, saying, "That's alright. What movie did you watch?"

Mom's response surprised me. She said, "You know what? I went to the movie theater, but I didn't actually watch a movie."

I decided to talk to her later the next day, but she called me first and shared the story of her movie theater experience.

"So, I went to the theater and bought a ticket. But then I realized I had an hour before the movie started. That's when I noticed a small coffee shop serving mint tea in golden teapots. I wanted to try some, so I sat by the window and asked the young man there for one of those teapots. He introduced himself and asked where I was from, and that's how our conversation started," She said.

"It turned out that the young man owned the teashop with his two brothers in a narrow streets of small Mediterranean town, next to the movie theater. We talked about their business and the beauty of the city. Then he shared something interesting. He said he had lost the taste for life and for all the joy and beauty in the world since his mother passed away."

Mom asked him how long ago she died; he said five years. Surprised, she asked, "Five years and you still can't find happiness?" He sadly replied, "No, I don't think I'll ever experience joy or happiness again. That's it for me." Mom encouraged him to sit down and talk.

She saw the conversation as a challenge, a case where she could help this person recover and reclaim his life. Mom asked if he knew that his mother's soul had gone to a beautiful place, filled with serenity and peace.

She knew he must have heard the same sentiment from others, but she wanted him to imagine the concept for himself. Mom described the image of his mother's body being like a dress she took off, and how her soul had flown away to a peaceful and gorgeous place.

He closed his eyes and replaced the image of burying his mother with the image of her soul finding bliss. When he opened his eyes, his face had changed. The sadness had lifted, and his eyes sparkled. In that moment, he finally allowed himself to let go and believe that his mother was in a much better place, giving himself permission to move on.

Mom asked him if he would rather have his mother come back to her sick body only to be with him. He firmly replied, "No, no, no. I want her to be where she is now, at rest and serene."

His despair was all about an idea he held onto, thinking he could never be happy after his mother's death. Once he let go of that idea, he freed himself from its grip.

"Always try to stay connected and in touch with your positive imagination," Mom told him. "There will be times when you feel down and revisit the pain of your mother's death. Those images might haunt you and create more damaging thoughts. But in those moments, acknowledge what's happening, then plug into your positive energy. Use your imagination to fight those negative thoughts and imagine your mother in a happy place, in the most positive state. Stay connected to your best energy."

This conversation happened more than ten years ago, but its impact remains with Mom and I. It taught us the power of letting go and finding happiness even in the face of loss.

Whenever life brings us down, we'll acknowledge those difficult moments and then tap into our positive energy. We'll fight off depressing thoughts by imagining our loved ones in a happier place, embracing the most upbeat state of being. Together, we'll navigate life's challenges and keep our spirits bright.

" Always stay connected and in touch with your positive imagination. **"**

Taking Control Over Feelings: Connecting To The Source of Positivity

It was a rough day. I was feeling out of control, with so much to do and not enough time to get it all done. Thoughts swirled around in my head, bumping into each other and I felt chaotic from the inside out. Mom caught me in this bad mood and knew something was wrong. She asked, "What's the matter, dear?"

I replied, "I have so many plans and things popping up that need my attention. It's making me unable to enjoy what's around me."

Mom said, "Don't let your feelings manipulate you, and don't let them take over you. Take control over them to prevent the mess and chaos of your thoughts. Keep close to your source of positive energy. As long as you stay connected to your source, you will gain control over your life. Once you drift away from your source, you lose control. So, plug in with the power of your source of positive energy."

Curious, I asked, "How should I connect to the source?"

Mom replied, "Stop for a moment, pause what you're doing, and take a deep breath. Connect with the inside of you, feel the breath coming inside of you as you breathe in. Then, you will feel a glimpse of peace. Once you sense that inner peace, you are connected."

As Mom described the process of plugging into the source of positive energy, I couldn't help but visualize how powerful and transformative this connection truly is.

Conversations with Mom: Recipes for Self-Help

Intentions Before Ingredients: Refocus When Things Go Wrong

Mom and I were in the kitchen. She was busy preparing a mouthwatering dish called Koshari, a popular Egyptian street food. My taste buds tingled in anticipation for the finished product. As she soaked the brown lentils and cooked the rice, she paused and said, "Let's talk about intentions."

I looked up from the cutting board where I was carefully chopping onions. Curious I asked, "Intentions? What do you mean, Mom?"

She smiled warmly. "Well, before diving into any task or adventure, it's important to set our intentions. It's like adding a special flavor to our actions, making them more meaningful and enjoyable."

I nodded, intrigued. "Can you give me an example?"

Mom began telling me a story about two weddings she had attended. "One wedding was all about showing off wealth and trying to outshine others. But you know what? It turned out to be the most boring wedding ever. On the other hand, there was a wedding at the beginning of the year where the intention was to bring family and friends together, treat them to delicious food, and create wonderful memories. And you know what? It was a joyful celebration, full of beauty and love."

I continued chopping onions as Mom prepared the tomato sauce for the Koshari. "Intentions really make a difference, don't they?" I asked.

Mom nodded, her hands skillfully moving. "Absolutely. They play a crucial role in our endeavors. Whether we're starting a new job, organizing a party, or even cooking a meal, we should always ask ourselves, 'Why am I doing this?' Is it for the right reasons? Is it to bring happiness and goodness to others?"

As the aroma of caramelized onions filled the kitchen, Mom began layering the rice, lentils, topping it with onions, tomato sauce, and the elbow pasta in a serving bowl. She scooped a generous portion onto my plate and said, "You know, the process becomes smoother and more joyful when our intentions are based on love."

I took a bite of the delicious Koshari, savoring the flavors. "That makes sense. But what if things go wrong along the way?" I asked.

Mom smiled knowingly. "Ah, that's when we need to pause and reevaluate our intentions. Sometimes, we encounter hiccups and difficulties, but by resetting our intentions, we can navigate through them. It's like recalibrating our compass to stay on the right path."

I recalled a recent baking mishap I had experienced. "You know, Mom, I was making a birthday cake for my daughter, and everything seemed to go wrong. The cream split, the cake layers turned out uneven, and the icing ended up a completely different color. I felt like a baking disaster."

Mom listened with empathy. "Oh, I've been there. But what did you do next?"

I took a deep breath, remembering the moment. "I stepped back, closed my eyes, and thought about why I was making that cake. I realized it wasn't about impressing others or meeting expectations. It was about seeing my daughter's face light up with joy and creating sweet moments for everyone to enjoy."

A smile tugged at the corners of Mom's lips. "And what happened then?"

With renewed determination, I continued, "I returned to the cake, pouring love and passion into every step. And you know what? The cake turned out to be a masterpiece, delighting everyone who tasted it."

Mom sat down to join me in appreciating the flavors of the Koshari, and she concluded, "Remember, before starting any project, before even gathering your ingredients, set your intentions. Intention is the secret ingredient that makes life more flavorful and fulfilling."

We shared a meaningful moment, appreciating the power of intentions in shaping our experiences and bringing joy to our endeavors.

Observe Without Judgment: Everyone Has an Emotional Journey

One morning I was struggling with a difficulty I couldn't seem to find a solution to. I called Mom, eager to share the concern about my child. "Mom," I began, "I love having our friends who moved from overseas so nearby. It's great that they settled only an hour away from us. But here's the issue: my three-year-old toddler has developed a strong attachment to their six-year-old daughter. She imitates her in every way, but the girl is only interested in my eleven-month-old baby. She treats her like a baby doll. It's adorable, but the behavior triggers my toddler's jealousy. She becomes demanding, seeking more attention from the girl and growing even more jealous of her baby sister. As a result, we end up with tantrums and a loss of control every time we hang out with our family friends."

Mom listened attentively before offering her perspective. "I think you might be over-analyzing and allowing your emotions to get the best of you," she said calmly. "Sometimes, we need to let things unfold without attaching too many emotions to them. Let's talk today about observing our feelings."

Curious, I asked Mom what happens when we observe our emotions and feelings. "It's simple," she explained. "They tend to dissipate. That's why we need to take a magnifying lens and identify each emotion we experience. I spent an entire year in a beach house, facing the ocean, reflecting solely on my feelings of shame. It required time, meditation, and a deep understanding of the emotions we carry. By looking them in the eye, we can eventually let them go."

She continued, focusing on the emotion of shame. "Shame is inherent in every human being. The experience originated with Adam and Eve when they ate the apple and felt ashamed before God. They became aware of their nakedness. That's how we feel when we experience shame. Imagine carrying that feeling of exposure constantly; that's what happens if we don't let go of shame. We can take the time to look at each emotion directly, one by one, and release them. It's a lengthy process, but the rewards are liberating."

Mom went on to ask me what happens when we observe the emotions of others. "Attempting to assume someone else's emotional burdens weighs us down," she said. "We can never truly know what they are feeling. So, it's important to focus on observing our own emotions rather than fixating on the feelings of others. When it comes to your daughters, avoid over-analyzing or assuming their emotions. Be empathetic without immersing yourself in someone else's feelings. Keep them separate from your own for the sake of your emotional hygiene and sanity."

She emphasized that criticism or judgment stems from ignorance. "We must reach a point where we don't judge others, not even our own children. A conscious person understands there is always more to a story than meets the eye. They recognize that there are multiple sides to every situation and that they will never know all of them. The more we learn, the more we realize how much we don't know. If we catch ourselves passing judgment on others or situations, we must acknowledge our ignorance."

With that in mind, Mom urged me to revisit the situation. "Learn to let it unfold naturally, without attaching judgments or excessive emotions," she advised. "Children are learning to experience and navigate their emotions. Allow your daughter to feel her jealousy and learn how to handle it. You can guide her by setting boundaries for tantrums, ensuring she doesn't hurt anyone or throw things. Apart from that, let the kids be kids and learn to take their own emotional journeys. And, my dear, find joy in each situation. I know it can be stressful at times, but practice observing without judgment."

I nodded, realizing the truth in my mother's words. "You're right," I admitted. "I want my kids to experience all their emotions, even the negative ones. I can't shield them from everything. Instead, I should teach them how to handle what they feel."

I could hear the smile in my mom's voice as she replied, "That's the spirit. It takes practice, but you'll get there. Embrace the role of guiding your children and fostering their emotional growth. And remember, observation without judgment is key."

"

Be empathetic without immersing yourself in someone else's feelings.

"

Controlling Our Doorknobs: Embrace the Cocktail Of Life

It was a dreary Friday afternoon in January. The sky wore a gray blanket, mirroring my gloomy mood. I made myself a cup of tea and settled down in my favorite chair as my baby played in the next room. Needing a distraction, I decided to call my sister.

She eagerly shared stories of her new friend and even sent me a video from a recent New Year's party. Among the crowd, one person stood out—a man with a cocktail in his hand, basking in the joy of the moment. He had a wide smile and moved in rhythmic dancing seeming to embody a deep sense of peace.

I watched the video repeatedly, trying to absorb and understand his genuine enjoyment. It dawned on me that it had been a long time since I felt that kind of harmony and tranquility. Being fully present in the moment and savoring it seemed like a distant memory.

As parents, our minds are often preoccupied with the future—thinking about meals, changing diapers, and preparing for various tasks. We also find ourselves dwelling on the past, analyzing the causes of illnesses, or regretting missed opportunities. Our thoughts become consumed with obligations, should-haves, and must-dos. Amidst this chaos, how can we grab life's metaphorical cocktail, surrender to the rhythm of the present, and truly relish the beauty around us?

I voiced this question to Mom, seeking her wisdom. She responded with a message, discussing the importance of control.

"When our internal control weakens, the outside world appears to slip from our grasp," she said. "We often believe we can control external circumstances, expending our energy trying to manipulate people and situations. However, we forget that true control starts within.

"Real control lies in managing our emotions and feelings. The more we become aware that control originates from within, the more we can direct that action with intention. It's like holding the doorknob to our inner selves. By regulating our emotions, thoughts, and feelings, the outside world begins to align with our desires.

"But controlling our thoughts is an ongoing process, like a wheel that keeps spinning endlessly. Although the wheel never stops, we have the power to steer the motion in the direction we choose. How? By increasing our awareness and consciously observing the wheel's movements. When our self-awareness falters, we become fixated on controlling the external world, unknowingly letting it influence our inner state, losing ourselves in the process.

"Let me give you an example. Imagine someone who watches the news, unaware of their emotional state. They become depressed and easily affected by negative events, falling ill simply by absorbing the depressing energy from the outside world. It's like leaving the doors to their inner selves wide open.

"Learning to open and close these inner doors is a skill we must acquire. The doorknobs are in our hands, but we must first become aware of them.

"Some people have lost their doorknobs altogether, leaving their doors perpetually open, allowing everything and anything to enter their lives. The outside world controls them. They are deeply affected by news and external events, unable to filter out the negative influences.

"On the other hand, some people always keep their doors closed. They may find happiness, but they risk isolating themselves from the world's suffering. It's an extreme approach that hampers their harmony with the external world.

"The most powerful and aware individuals are those who have control over the doorknobs to their inner selves. They can open and close the doors as they please, deciding when to let the outside world in and when to retreat to their inner peace.

In this state of heightened awareness, they acknowledge the world's suffering, empathizing with those in pain. Yet, they also know when to lock their doors, retreating to their own inner serenity as needed.

"If we strive to attain this state, we can live in harmony with the universe. We'll be able to grasp that metaphorical cocktail and enjoy life, pursuing the highest goals of love, joy, and happiness. No matter what happens outside, our inner peace and joy remain unaffected."

"

When our internal control weakens, the outside world appears to slip from our grasp, we often believe we can control external circumstances, expending our energy trying to manipulate people and situations. However, we forget that true control starts within.

"

Embracing Uniqueness: Don't Let Comparison Prohibit Your Imagination

I sat down as Mom brought me a cup of butter mint tea, joining me and the kids, who were absorbed in their own imaginative play. As she handed me the cup, she smiled and said, "Let me tell you a story." It was a moment that felt warm and comforting, the perfect setting for a tale to unfold.

Mom began. "When I was an elementary school teacher, I was often faced with criticism from my supervisors for not incorporating comparison-based teaching methods. They believed that children should learn through comparing things, but I strongly disagreed, I felt that approach limited their understanding."

Reflecting on those teaching days, she explained, "supervisors from the Ministry of Education would visit our classrooms and provide feedback. Every time, I received the same comment, 'You don't use comparison methods.' But I firmly believed that when discussing fruits, for example, it was important to appreciate the distinct vitamins, textures, and characteristics of each fruit. Why force unnecessary comparisons?"

Comparison methods, Mom explained, are deeply embedded in our society, from early education all the way to higher levels. Curious, I asked her why she opposed the theory. "What harm does it do?" I wondered, trying to find a common ground using the analogy of jigsaw puzzle pieces. To complete the picture, you must compare the pieces to find the ones that fit together.

With a gentle smile, Mom replied, "But why limit our thinking to mere comparisons? Why confine ourselves to squares when there's a whole world of possibilities?"

She then took me on a journey back to a memory of a family trip. "When you and your brothers and sister were young, we traveled to the mountains of Indonesia. When we arrived, we realized we'd come in the middle of the rainy season. We found ourselves cooped up inside the villa.

I seized the opportunity to let your imaginations run wild. Every piece of furniture became a magical prop in your games: chairs transformed into supermarket cashiers, footrests turned into hospital beds, and the rug became a vast sea with the tiles as the shores.

Watching you kids unleash your boundless creativity and witnessing how you took the ordinary and made it extraordinary, left me marveling at the power of vivid imagination to create endless fun and exploration. We didn't need external toys."

I interjected, pointing out that things changed once we started school and learned to compare. Mom's response struck a chord with me. "Be unique," she said emphatically. "Don't copy people. Avoid comparing your situation with that of others. Comparison restricts our true potential and limits what we can achieve in this world. However, don't think you're too special or different either; that will only lead to sameness."

In conclusion, Mom was saying we should embrace our uniqueness, freeing ourselves from the confines of comparison and nurturing our individuality. Just as we discovered during our rainy mountain trip, the power of imagination knows no bounds. So let us not compare, but instead, celebrate the endless possibilities that lie within us all.

As the story came to an end, Mom and I exchanged knowing glances, understanding the profound message she had conveyed. We sipped our tea, appreciating the warmth and love that filled the room. In that moment, I felt a renewed sense of purpose, a commitment to live a life driven by my own unique path. With Mom's guidance, I knew that I could navigate the world, unburdened by comparison and ready to embrace the limitless opportunities that lay ahead.

"

Be unique. Don't copy people. Avoid comparing your situation with that of others. Comparison restricts our true potential and limits what we can achieve in this world.

"

Unpacking Emotions: Embracing Individuality

As I set down a tray with a freshly brewed cup of coffee, two slices of toasted bread, homemade blueberry jam, and butter, I felt the urge to share my thoughts with Mom. Sitting across from her, I expressed my longing to write a book, despite not considering myself a skilled writer or being confident with my words. The presence of my two young children also made me doubt whether I had the time to pursue such a project.

Mom, ever understanding, suggested we unpack these emotions. She grabbed a pen and paper, ready to delve into the heart of the matter. "Let's talk about these obstacles you've set for yourself," she said, with a knowing smile.

"So, you feel you're not good with words and doubt your abilities, unlike other writers," Mom began with gentle reassurance. "Let's start by addressing the problem of comparison. When we compare ourselves to others, the struggle becomes a losing battle. The struggle breeds negative emotions and undermines our self-worth."

I nodded, taking in her wisdom. "That's a profound way to look at it, Mom. We really are distinct individuals with unique fingerprints."

"Exactly!" Mom exclaimed, her eyes shining with enthusiasm. "Each person's fingerprint is completely different. No two fingerprints have ever been found to be identical. That's a message from the creator, reminding us that despite our outward similarities, we are all inherently different. Eliminate comparison and celebrate individuality."

Feeling encouraged, I said, "You make a good point, Mom, but what about the issue of time? I don't have time to write this book. Plus, society operates on schedules and deadlines."

Mom leaned back in her chair. "Time is a concept we create for ourselves. While there are societal constraints, it's important not to let time control us entirely. Yes, it's necessary to follow certain schedules, like grocery shopping during open hours or attending appointments. But when it comes to personal tasks and goals, a flexible mindset is essential.

"Creating a daily plan with timelines is perfectly fine but remember you set those milestones for yourself. If you can't meet a self-imposed deadline, don't stress about it. Be open to possibilities and adjust to what works best for you. Trust that time will flow as it should, without unnecessary stress."

I nodded, absorbing her words. The idea that time didn't have to be a rigid ruler governing every aspect of my life felt liberating. I realized I could find a balance between honoring commitments and allowing room for my passions and dreams.

"Ultimately," Mom concluded, "the purpose of our existence is to live in joy, love, and happiness. We must do our part and let go of the rest, trusting in a higher power. We can't control every aspect of our lives."

She shared a story about the Virgin Mary, who was asked to shake a palm tree while in labor. The task seemed impossible, but Mary touched the tree and the dates came to her, easing her labor. Mom drew a parallel to our own lives—take action, shake the metaphorical palm tree, but also let go of control and have faith that things will work out.

As I enjoyed the last sip of my coffee, I felt a newfound sense of hope and determination. Mom's guidance had provided the perspective and encouragement I needed to pursue my dreams without succumbing to comparison or being enslaved by time. With her wisdom echoing in my heart, I embraced the path ahead, ready to embark on my writing journey, trusting in my own voice and the timing of the universe.

" the **purpose** of our existence is to live in joy, love, and happiness. "

Conquering The Enemy Within: Re-organizing The Mind

Mom had just brewed fresh mint tea and prepared a Middle Eastern breakfast on small plates. She placed pita bread in the bread basket, feta cheese topped with olive oil and za'atar on another plate, and butter and apricot jam in yet another small dish.

Mom held a coffee mug with the words, "I'm a Mom. What's your superpower?" emblazoned on it.

"When faced with a choice between a piece of fruit and a chocolate bar, we often find ourselves reaching for the chocolate, even though we know the fruit is a healthier option," Mom said. "Why do we do that?

"Deep within us resides a foe that leads us to make poor decisions like choosing chocolate over fruit. We have the power to tame this ever-present enemy of the self just as we control our thoughts, understanding that some drag us into negativity and misfortune, while others bring joy and success."

Curiously, I asked, "How can we overcome this enemy?"

We stepped into the messy playroom as we continued our conversation. Books, stuffed animals, and building blocks were strewn all over the floor, making it difficult to walk.

Mom replied to my inquiry with enthusiasm. "That's the question we need to focus on. Our liberations lie in the answer.

"First, we must acknowledge and be aware of the enemy's existence. Once we recognize that, we can ask ourselves the right questions and discipline our foe, preventing its harmful influence. When we are connected to our source, experiencing positive emotions and energy, we weaken the enemy. However, when that link grows thin, the enemy gains strength and takes control.

"Awareness is key. We need to pay attention not only to the enemy's presence but also to the ongoing conversation between our self and that enemy. By observing and directing this conversation, we can gain control. It's a gradual process, but with practice, the work becomes easier."

In that moment, as I tidied up the playroom, organizing the toys, blocks, and stuffed animals, I felt a sense of relief. The books found their place on the shelf, and the little play kitchen was clean and ready for the kids to pretend to cook in again.

Mom likened meditation to the act of organizing the mind and taming the self-enemy, just like I had organized the playroom.

The exercise brings order to our thoughts and reduces the self-enemy's grip.

Before practicing meditation and mindfulness my mind was cluttered, making it hard to find a clear thought or idea. But as I made space and brought order to my mind, the self-enemy's influence lessened. It became easier to make wise decisions and to find myself amidst the chaos.

Now, before making choices, I often ask myself, "Where is this coming from? Is it the self-enemy or the peaceful and mindful self?" These simple questions help me discern and make decisions aligned with my true self.

That breakfast felt like a warm hug. Now, I need to start my morning chores.

"before making choices, I often ask myself, Where is this coming from? Is it the self-enemy or the peaceful and mindful self? These simple questions help me discern and make decisions aligned with my true self."

The Power Of Gratitude: Glowing From The Inside Out

As I observed my Mom preparing her favorite homemade facemask, I marveled at her flawless skin. Taking care of her complexion was one of her passions, and she had perfected a radiant and softening facemask recipe over the years.

Mom mixed dry oats, plain yogurt, and honey in a bowl, applying the mask carefully. Sitting with her face up, she warned me not to let the mask drip. I hesitated, unsure if I should try it too.

Sensing my hesitation, Mom asked, "Have you decided if you want one?" I politely declined and sat down.

Mom said: "do you know that a grateful state of mind attracts more blessings, contentment, and abundance? It is the highest mental state, where we feel satisfied and thankful. On the contrary, covering up blessings through complaining or dwelling on negativity tortures the soul. In this state, the mind veils the blessings until they become invisible, leading to suffering, depression, and negative consequences."

Curiously, I asked Mom how we can enter this elevated state of gratitude?She responded, comparing the task to a muscle that needs exercise. "It's a simple yet consistent practice. With attention and energy gratitude grows stronger and bigger. The more we embrace gratefulness and complain less, the more we attract beautiful things," she said.

If we find ourselves complaining, covering up the blessings, Mom advised that we pause, reconsider, and reset our inner state to one of gratitude. She emphasized the importance of engaging in acts that foster gratitude, such as kindness, prayer, connecting with the source, expressing thanks to others, motivating friends, or helping someone in need.

"These acts bring us into the state of gratefulness, where joy flourishes. Conversely, when we complain, we cover up the blessings, losing joy and experiencing negative emotions," Mom explained.

I asked about stress, which she clarified was another way of covering up blessings. "Focusing on something gives it energy and amplifies its impact. For instance, when a baby cries, our stress arises because we focus on the crying. However, shifting our focus to finding a solution directs energy toward the resolution, enabling us to enjoy the process and energize the solution rather than the problem. Energy follows our focus," Mom enlightened me.

Mom went to wash her face, her skin glowing. She asked if I wanted to try the mask, and I decided to give it a go, hoping for a similar radiant result. As she applied the mask, I felt a sense of gratitude for the moment, realizing that cultivating a grateful mindset brings about positivity and beauty not only in our skin but also to life as a whole.

"

Focusing on something gives it energy and **amplifies** its impact.

"

Laughter Is The Sweetness Of Life's Cake: Don't Be So Serious

Mom came into the kitchen and found me busy with my usual multitasking. In my mind, I had already decided to prepare basmati rice, green beans with beef, and salad for lunch. However, I also wanted to make my favorite apple cake. My thoughts were all over the place.

Mom's intuition kicked in. "I feel like we haven't laughed in a while. What's going on?" she asked.

Catching her gaze, my brow furrowed in deep concentration. "You know what? I just noticed the frown on my face, and it made me ponder why genuine laughter has been absent from my life lately," I told her.

With a desire to address the underlying matter, Mom suggested, "Let's have a conversation about seriousness, but first let's come to a shared understanding of what I mean by 'serious.' I'm referring to the qualities of being rigid, unchangeable, strict, and severe.

"Picture seriousness as an eraser that has the power to eliminate love, fun, and joy. The opposite of seriousness, however, doesn't entail being frivolous, lazy, or inattentive. Instead, it revolves around the concept of avoiding neglectfulness.

"Some people are afraid of being seen as neglectful or insubstantial, so they take away the playful side of life and miss all the best parts. It's like making an apple cake and forgetting to add the yogurt, milk, or cream—the result will be hard and difficult to swallow.

"We need moisture in the batter of life to make our days light, easy to enjoy, and digest. That moistness consists of kindness, love, flexibility, easiness, and laughter. If you approach life with too much seriousness, you'll lose out on the enjoyable aspects."

Mom asked if I understood, and I nodded with a shy smile. She said, "Okay, let's check on the cake."

I took the apple cake out of the oven and flipped it onto the cooling rack. As the sweet-apple aroma filled the room, I sprinkling some powdered sugar on top. We both looked at the cake and burst into laughter knowing the confection wouldn't last long.

Laughter Is The Sweetness Of Life's Cake

"

We need moisture in the batter of life to make our days light, easy to enjoy, and digest. That moistness consists of kindness, love, flexibility, easiness, and laughter.

The Head Of and The Tail Of Beliefs: Do A Spring Cleaning Of The Mind

My mom possesses an incredible talent for whipping up rice dishes in mere minutes. She's undoubtedly one of the quickest cooks I know, second only to her older sister who effortlessly prepares meals in what seems like a fraction of a second. Their culinary prowess amazes me. Their lightning-fast cooking skills may have been honed from the necessity of feeding their large families, each with five children.

As Mom started to make an Arabic dish called Kabsa, she rinsed the white basmati rice, then she swiftly grabbed a cutting board and began chopping garlic and onions. At the same time, she sliced the chicken breast into medium pieces and asked me to fetch a can of tomato paste from the pantry.

In a flash, she retrieved the Dutch oven, put it on the stove, and turned the heat to high. Adding olive oil to the pot, she tossed in the onions, garlic, and the sliced chicken, followed by two tablespoons of tomato paste. After a good mix, she added a blend of Arabian spices, including cloves, cumin, turmeric, and bay leaves. A pinch of salt and pepper and a cup of water joined the mixture, which she promptly covered.

Meanwhile, with her other hand, she put the rice in a separate pot, and added water, salt, and a spoonful of butter. Covering it as well, she set the stove to medium, turned around, with a teacup in one hand, and set another on the table for me. "Let's talk about beliefs," she said.

Mom shared a story with me. "There was a woman who had a peculiar habit while cooking fish. Every time she prepared fish, she always cut off the tail and head. One day, her curious daughter asked, 'Why do you always remove the tail and head of the fish?'

"The mother replied, 'Well, my own mother always cooked fish this way.' Intrigued, the girl asked her grandmother the same question. She explained that she learned the practice from her mother. Consulting other relatives, they eventually discovered that their great-grandmother had only one small pan that couldn't accommodate a whole fish. Hence, she trimmed the head and tail of every fish she cooked to fit in the pan."

Mom elaborated, "Beliefs are shaped by our experiences. Positive experiences create positive ideas, while negative experiences give rise to negative ones. But this isn't the ideal way to form beliefs."

Curious, I asked, "Well then, how should we create beliefs if not through experiences?"

Mom replied, "Beliefs can also be shaped by our thoughts. Our thoughts, emotions, and beliefs are like interconnected gears, each influencing the other. It all begins with our thoughts, which then generate feelings, and these feelings, in turn, shape our beliefs.

Therefore, it's essential to be mindful of our thoughts, observing them before they generate feelings and solidify into beliefs. By being aware of this process, we can actively choose empowering thoughts that lead to positive beliefs. To gain clarity and self-awareness, I suggest taking out a paper and pen occasionally to examine our beliefs—a sort of beliefs spring-cleaning that we should conduct at least once a season. It allows us to recognize beliefs that are important and serve us well, which we should cherish and nurture."

"How do we do a 'beliefs spring-cleaning?' How do we even know what our beliefs are?" I asked.

Mom replied, "with paper and pen, beliefs should be consciously created. Write down your beliefs, then trace each belief back to its roots by questioning our ideas. Why do we hold this belief? Just like the girl who questioned cutting the fish, ask yourself, did I develop this idea as the result of an experience? Was this belief inherited or copied? Did it stem from a specific event, was it from my thoughts?"

"Once we've questioned a belief, how do we change it?" I asked. "What if it turns out that the belief doesn't come from a conscious place?"

"In that case," Mom advised, "you need to revisit the belief. Try frying the fish with the head and tail intact and see how it turns out."

Reflecting on my own beliefs, I said, "Like my ideas about bananas. I have an aversion to them—I dislike the smell, taste, texture, and even their color."

"That belief stems from a past experience," Mom said. "When you were little, you accidentally left a banana in your backpack. We discovered it a week later, rotten and repulsive. You were so disgusted you threw up. That experience shaped your belief."

I laughed and admitted, "Even now, I can't bring myself to touch a banana."

"Let's try a different perspective on bananas," Mom suggested. "Consider their nutritional benefits, like how they're rich in potassium and magnesium. They're a great snack that can uplift your mood.

"Consider other examples, like someone who claims, 'I'm not good at school. I've never been good.' Consequently, they give up on their education due to a single bad grade or a failed class. They develop the belief that school isn't meant for them. Similarly, a person who endures a painful breakup or divorce might believe they're inept at relationships, leading them to fear meeting new people or going on dates.

"It is important to question our beliefs, particularly the significant ones that hinder our progress or prevent us from letting go. To enhance your personal growth and self-reflection, I suggest engaging in a helpful practice. Find a serene spot where you can sit alone with a pen and paper, allowing yourself to thoroughly explore and assess your beliefs. Begin by jotting down the phrase, 'I believe that...' and see where your thoughts take you. Take your time to uncover your beliefs and understand their origins.

"As you explore each belief in greater depth, consider whether any of them hold negative connotations or limit your potential.

If you identify such beliefs, take the opportunity to challenge and replace them with fresh perspectives. Embrace the chance to approach these replaced beliefs with renewed curiosity and open-mindedness.

"By engaging in this introspective exercise, you open doors to personal growth, allowing yourself the opportunity to evolve and be open to more empowering beliefs. Embracing fresh perspectives and giving experiences another try can lead to transformation and a greater sense of fulfillment in your life's journey."

The enticing aroma of rice and the tantalizing spices used to cook the chicken filled the air. Mom added the rice to the chicken mixture after reducing the water, deftly stirring the dish with a fork. We set the table and prepared a green salad. Finally, we sat down, and Mom declared, "Let's eat."

As we started the meal, she said, "What we've discussed are only small examples of how beliefs are intertwined with life experience. However, when we consider the significant idea that can shape our lives, such as the belief that weight gain is solely related to trapped emotions, or that past failures discourage us from even attempting new relationships, we realize the profound impact our thoughts can have."

As we savored our meal, the culmination of my mom's culinary expertise and our insightful conversation overwhelmed me. I realized the depth of the connection between beliefs and experiences. The notion of questioning our opinions, especially the ones that hinder our goals or hold us back, resonated with me. It became clear that revisiting beliefs, understanding their roots, and embracing new perspectives should be an ongoing practice.

With each bite of the flavorful Kabsa, I felt a renewed sense of empowerment, knowing I hold the key to unlocking new paths in my journey.

The Flow Of Your Rivers: Avoid Resistance

On the eve of the Lunar New Year, our family follows a tradition of making white food or beverages to symbolize good luck, purity, and prosperity.

One year, Mom prepared a traditional Arabian delicacy known as Sahlab, also called "kahwa laws," a warm drink and dessert combined in a single cup. It is made by blending almond flour, cornstarch, and sugar with milk, resulting in a thick consistency. To enhance the flavor and texture, the drink is garnished with roasted almonds, pistachios, and coconut.

Mom prepared two mugs and handed one to me. We settled on the balcony, wrapped in blankets, gazing at the twinkling stars while enjoying the comforting warmth of the drink. It felt like a loving embrace from our ancestors.

Looking up at the stars, Mom shared her wisdom: "When we fixate on negative emotions, feelings, or circumstances in life, we create resistance."

"Resistance to what?" I wondered.

"Imagine yourself walking against the flow of a river. After a while, exhaustion sets in, and you become oblivious to the beauty surrounding you because your sole focus is on battling the current.

"Similarly, when we concentrate on negative emotions or our own shortcomings, it engenders pain, dissatisfaction, troubles, and sadness," Mom answered.

She glanced upwards, her eyes closing momentarily, and then she spoke with conviction. "Let us make a vow at the start of this year to always walk in alignment with the natural flow of our rivers."

Her words hung in the air, carrying a profound sense of purpose and determination.

As we sat there, under the gentle embrace of the night sky, a renewed sense of harmony settled within us. We knew that by choosing to navigate our rivers in harmony with their flow, we would find greater fulfillment, joy, and contentment.

The Flow Of Your Rivers

"

Imagine yourself walking against the flow of a river. After a while, exhaustion sets in, and you become oblivious to the beauty surrounding you because your sole focus is on battling the current. Similarly, when we concentrate on negative emotions or our own shortcomings, it engenders pain, dissatisfaction, troubles, and sadness.

Following Mama Duck: Parents Program Their Children

O n a refreshing spring morning, Mom and I took my baby for a stroll. Equipped with a blanket, teething toys, and snacks, we headed toward the nearby lake.

We spread the blanket on the ground on the soft grass beneath a tree. Three small, black ducks gracefully trailing behind their mother captured our attention. In an instant, the mother duck leapt into the lake, and the ducklings, one by one, eagerly followed her into the chilly water.

Mom and I shared a hearty laugh, thoroughly charmed by the adorable spectacle we had just witnessed in nature. Taking a deep breath, Mom turned to me, her gaze filled with wisdom, and said,

"The role of parents is truly significant. I want you to know that the mind can receive negative, positive, or balanced programming.

"Natural human programming includes negative components such as fear and selfishness, which are inherent to our survival needs. These existing programs can be amplified or reduced through reprogramming by parents."

"My baby and toddler cry every time we are in the elevator, even though they have no negative past experiences," I said. "Why are they terrified of something they haven't encountered before?"

"That is survival mode. Being in a closed space carries the danger of losing oxygen," Mom replied.

She continued, "When we are out of balance, and when negative emotions outweigh the positive ones in our daily lives, we tend to become unhappy for extended periods. We may develop phobias and anxiety that hinder our ability to carry out our daily activities with serenity. In these situations, we are far from the paths of peace, love, and joy. This is the negative programming.

"We need to understand that the mind can be reprogrammed, and we must be willing to act. We can measure the maturity and awareness of individuals by observing how they respond to their negative emotions. Do they blame others? Do they blame themselves? Or do they pause, self-evaluate, and make changes?

"Let's return to the role of parents in raising children who are conscious of their feelings and behaviors. Parents should strive to enhance the goodness in our nature, such as generosity and sharing, while reducing negative survival instincts like fear, selfishness, and guilt. The responsibility of conscious parents is to program, reprogram, and continually program again."

Mom stopped and gave the baby a teething cookie to suck on. We both watched the ducks cross the lake and climb out again. "Everything we talk about leads to liberation from yourself, from your thoughts, and takes you to positive mental places," Mom said. "Keep our conversations as a reference in your life and always come back to them. We have discussed several topics. Whenever you feel the need to revisit our conversation, soak in the information, meditate on it, and apply what you've learned."

Mom explained that the practices of programming and reprogramming are skills. She acknowledged that it may not be easy, but with practice, they can become ingrained behaviors. Over time, they become part of the subconscious and are applied automatically.

Curious, I asked, "How will I know when the behaviors of my children have become skills?"

Mom replied without hesitation, "Once they become their normal behaviors, then you will know you have successfully applied positive programming. Let's go for a walk."

As we strolled around the lake, my baby said "duck" for the first time. We both stopped and laughed. I couldn't resist picking up my daughter from her stroller, showering her with hugs and kisses, and my heart was filled with joy.

"

When we are out of **balance**, and when negative emotions outweigh the positive ones in our daily lives, we tend to become unhappy for extended periods. We may develop phobias and anxiety that hinder our ability to carry out our daily activities with serenity. In these situations, we are far from the paths of peace, love, and joy.

"

Shaping The Life We Desire: Exploring Feelings, Emotions, and Passion

As Mom exercised on the treadmill, wearing a homemade masks and donning towel-wrapped hair, she posed a thought-provoking question, "Do you know the difference between feelings, emotions, and passion?"

"I haven't really thought about it much before," I answered honestly.

"Feelings are small things that come and go, beyond our control. They can be good or bad, and sometimes they don't even have a reason. Emotions can have a lasting impact on us, shaping our lives for better or worse. They can make us feel positive or negative, influencing our outlook on things.

"Passion, however, is a controlled emotion. You are have it intentionally when you start doing something you love. It brings immense joy and positive experiences. When someone is passionate about something, it's evident, and we love seeing it. Passion takes us to a higher level of positive emotions and opens doors to our dreams and desires. It's crucial to find our passion, pursue it, and always be enthusiastic about what we do.

"Dealing with emotions can be challenging. If we let them run wild, they become like an untamed bush that needs to be pruned and nurtured. We must learn to identify, name, and understand our emotions. Otherwise, we'll be like toddlers, overwhelmed and unable to express ourselves."

Mom paused for a drink of water and stepped off the treadmill. Looking at me, she asked, "Would you like to have control over your day?"

She mentioned the movie "50 First Dates" as an example of creating our daily experience. In the movie, the main character suffers from short-term memory loss and cannot remember the man she is dating, and even falls in love with. So, every morning, her partner has to remind her what her life is like and of who he is and that they are together. "The main character starts each day by setting her expectations and understanding her purpose," Mom said. "We can do the same by monitoring our thoughts, changing unhelpful beliefs, and controlling our emotions. By doing this, we can create a new reality and shape the life we desire everyday."

Mom explained the concept of a paradigm—an unconscious system that holds our beliefs and keeps us in our comfort zone. By understanding and adjusting our paradigm, we can achieve what we want. We must pay attention to our thoughts, identify negative patterns, and replace them with positive ones focused on happiness and laughter.

When Mom finished, she went to take a shower, leaving me to sort out the mental disarray her words caused. I needed to find a quiet place to unpack and process her profound insights, jotting them down, and, most importantly, figuring out how to apply them in my own life.

As Mom's voice faded, silence filled the room, allowing her words to settle within me. I realized that this conversation, like many others with Mom, was more than a passing exchange; it was a transformative moment, a seed of wisdom planted deep within my heart.

"

Dealing with emotions can be challenging. If we let them run wild, they become like an untamed bush that needs to be pruned and nurtured. We must learn to identify, name, and understand our emotions. Otherwise, we'll be like toddlers, overwhelmed and unable to express ourselves.

"

The Power Of Thoughts: Taking Control Of Your Mind

At one time, I was in a phase of life where I felt upset and frustrated all the time. It started when I moved into a new house, excited to make it my own. From the moment I stepped inside, I instantly fell in love with the place. It had everything I had ever dreamed of—a beautiful garden, spacious rooms, and a cozy atmosphere.

I poured my heart and soul into taking care of the house. It became more than just a rental to me; it felt like my own little sanctuary. I made sure it was always clean and well-maintained, treating it with the utmost respect. It felt like my home, and I wanted to make it a place I could be proud of.

Things took an unfortunate turn when it was time for me to move out. I had completed my lease agreement, and I eagerly awaited the return of my security deposit. To my dismay, the landlord refused to give it back without providing any valid reason.

I couldn't believe it. It felt incredibly unfair and unjust. I had taken such good care of the house, there was no reason to withhold my deposit. I had invested time and effort into making it beautiful and ensuring everything was in perfect order. The fact that my efforts were being disregarded left me feeling disheartened.

I struggled for a significant period to overcome the feeling of injustice. Every time thoughts of that house crossed my mind, or I happened to pass by the street it was located on, or even if I heard the landlord's name mentioned, I couldn't help but feel upset. The emotions associated with the situation seemed to linger and took considerable time to dissipate.

I decided I needed help from Mom. As I sat with her telling her about my feelings, a delightful aroma floated through the air, capturing my attention. In her hands, she carried a cup of, crafted from lightly roasted coffee beans.

This traditional beverage, brewed with water and infused with fragrant spices like cardamom, cloves, and saffron, promised to awaken my senses and to provide a moment of respite. To complement the exquisite flavor of the coffee, my Mom also presented a plate of dates.

This pairing formed a harmonious combination, as the natural sweetness of the dates beautifully balanced the subtle bitterness of the coffee. It was a delightful harmony of flavors, inviting me to savor each sip and to relish the companionship of my mom's thoughtful gesture.

Mom began, "You know that all people experience fluctuating feelings and emotions?"

"I know I do," I replied.

"There are people who possess complete control over their emotions and thoughts—these are what I call secure individuals. They remain positive because they are at peace and feel secure. Achieving this state requires practice and the ability to control one's thoughts," Mom continued.

"Understanding this concept is crucial. It involves programming our minds about how we think of others. Have you ever noticed feeling upset merely by thinking about someone with whom you have a negative connection?

"When you think of a person, you automatically create what I call an 'energy thread' between the two of you," Mom said. "If your beliefs about that person are positive, this thread carries positive energy, and just thinking about them can bring you positivity.

"Conversely, if your beliefs about someone are negative, or if they have had a negative impact on your life, you'll experience negative feelings and energy when you think of them.

"Therefore, conscious individuals can choose whom they think about and how. But what if thoughts of someone you've created a negative connection with keep appearing?

In such cases, you need to be aware that thinking about that person will only bring heartache.

"Instead, replace those thoughts with something you genuinely enjoy. It could be your favorite food, a beautiful memory, a satisfying accomplishment like organizing your closet, or even the anticipation of a delicious dinner. Repeatedly replacing thoughts of negative individuals with positive ones will develop a habit of diverting your mind and cutting the energy thread before it becomes stronger.

"This practice enables you to control your thoughts and the people you choose to focus on. When you think of someone you share positive experiences with, you feel good, and a positive energy thread builds up between you. The more you think of them, the more positive you feel. It all boils down to control and training your mind regarding those to whom you give your thoughts and those you don't."

I thought for a moment and then said, "Mom, sometimes it's inevitable to discuss someone I've had a negative experience with especially when I'm trying to solve a problem or work together."

Mom responded, "There's a difference between thinking about a person versus focusing on the processes and tasks you have to deal with together. For example, when dealing with someone you want to sue for not returning your deposit, you're contemplating the legal process, not thinking about their behavior.

"Your prepared, mindful self comes into play. Be conscious and aware of where your thoughts are heading and how long you dwell on that person. Treat the process like a file: open it, handle what you need, then close it and move on. Don't let handling the file become an ongoing obsession or leave that 'file' open on your mental desk. After discussing what is necessary, replace thoughts involving that person with something else. Training that control muscle in your brain is like going to the gym—the more you practice, the stronger and faster your reflexes become."

As we finished the last sip of coffee, I felt invigorated and ready for anything.

The Power Of Thoughts

Conversations with Mom: Recipes for Self-Help

Liberate And Love Yourself: You Are Complete

While Mom and I were in the kitchen, we decided to preparing a beloved Egyptian dish called Molokhia. This unique dish featured vibrant green leaves of a plant known as Jute, or Jews Mallow. Molokhia was not only delicious but also held a special place in our hearts, a reminder of our shared heritage and cherished family recipes.

As we gathered the ingredients, I couldn't help but admire the vibrant green color of the Molokhia leaves. They had a distinct earthy aroma that promised a delightful culinary adventure. Mom and I began washing and chopping the leaves, their crisp textures a testament to their freshness.

In a large pot, we simmered chicken broth, adding aromatic spices like garlic, coriander, and cumin to infuse the liquid with rich flavors. The scent that wafted from the pot was nothing short of intoxicating, filling the kitchen with warmth and anticipation.

With the Molokhia leaves prepared and the broth infused with flavor, we carefully added the greens to the simmering liquid. As they wilted into the broth, the transformation was mesmerizing. The dish began to take on the characteristic texture that made Molokhia so unique.

We served it over a bed of fluffy rice, the dark green Molokhia contrasting beautifully with the pristine white grains. The final touch was a drizzle of zesty lemon juice, adding a burst of freshness to each spoonful.

As we sat down to enjoy our meal, we savored each bite of the Molokhia. Mom recalled a story about a woman she knew who was deeply in love but faced a significant dilemma. The man she desired to marry and build a home with, to start a family, was already married and had children of his own.

"Why don't you get a divorce since you are so unhappy with your wife and start over?" the woman asked. He replied he wanted a mistress and nothing more. Even though he was cheating, he wanted to maintain his marriage and family.

The woman remained his mistress for many years until she met my mom and shared her story. Mom was surprised to see such a beautiful lady who ran her own successful business make such a poor choice in a man.

"You are being put to the test," Mom said. "You must choose higher, positive, enlightened power or follow dark, negative energy. Sometimes we are so deeply immersed in what we are doing that we can't see we are succumbing to the dark energy."

Mom told her she believed she deserved better. She had to decide whether to continue in a relationship that diminished her and had no future.

"You need to know that you are full and complete by yourself," Mom said. "There is no one and nothing out there that is supposed to complete you. You are born complete; with all the capacity and tools you need to live in harmony within yourself and be happy. You only need to discover and unlock those qualities because they are already within you."

Mom started seeing the woman more often and reminding her of her self-worth. One day, like removing a bandage, the woman realized that she no longer loved the man. She had created an illusion of a good man in her mind and embellished that creation with the idea of love.

Her self-awareness and self-love emerged. Once she started loving herself, she realized her worth far exceeded anything he could ever offer her. She left him; she couldn't bear the thought of him anymore and focused on expanding her business. Now, she is an even more successful entrepreneur who also loves herself.

Mom recounted this story and said to me, "Always remember that you are complete just the way you are. Within you lies the power to create your own happiness. You possess every capability needed to find fulfillment. It's essential to understand that no person, family, or material possession can truly complete you. While they can enhance your life, they are not the missing piece. This truth has been reiterated through countless stories of individuals tirelessly seeking external sources of happiness, only to discover that what they desired was within them all along. Remember this, and let it resonate within your being."

I glanced up at Mom, gratitude filling my eyes. "You're absolutely right," I admitted, feeling a sense of relief wash over me. "I just need to remind myself of this truth more often."

With a gentle smile, Mom nodded in agreement, knowing the power of this realization. We shared a moment of understanding, an unspoken pact to support each other on this journey of self-discovery and self-acceptance.

Desires Overwhelm the Mind: It's Time To Declutter

I have too many desires that keep me tossing and turning at night. I wanted to go on a trip, so naturally, I found myself knee-deep in a frantic search for flights to Miami. But then, as luck would have it, I stumbled upon a mesmerizing princess dress for my daughter, and suddenly, my desire to acquire it took over.

I scoured countless websites, comparing prices like a bargain-hunting ninja. Just when I thought I had it all figured out, I stumbled upon an apple cake recipe that triggered my desire to bake. Forget trips and dresses, it was time to whisk up a culinary showpiece!

Oh, but hold your spatulas, because amidst my baking extravaganza, I stumbled upon a craft idea for Mother's Day that had me envisioning an artistic masterpiece to impress my loved ones. Next thing you know, I'm daydreaming about turning those crafts into a thriving business.

I feverishly search how to obtain a business license and sell my creations online. And voila! Here I am, completely exhausted, with a mind cluttered by an army of unfulfilled desires. Who needs sleep when you can have a mental circus instead?

Mom brought a basket of freshly washed laundry and sat down to start folding. She said, "Sometimes, we need to let go of our desires. They can be dangerous for us. They can ruin our lives if we connect our happiness and joy to them. When we can't fulfill our many desires, we might feel sad and discouraged, forgetting about all the blessings we already have.

"Our brains can become addicted to wanting more and more, and the situation becomes overwhelming. Even if we achieve a desire, we lose the pleasure we expected because our brain has already created new desires in the meantime. It's like a never-ending cycle, with one desire leading to another, and so on. As a result, no matter how much we acquire, we still aren't happy because our brain becomes addicted to desiring something we don't have."

I began folding the clothes with Mom. "How can we break this cycle of constantly creating desires? How can we learn to be content with what we already have?" I asked.

"Let me explain the difference between intentions and desires," Mom responded. "When we want to accomplish something, we need intentions, not only desires. Intentions involve focusing on the process and taking organized steps towards achieving our goals. By setting intentions, we approach tasks with a balanced mindset, knowing that the process itself is important in reaching our desired outcome.

"For example, let's say you have the intention to go on vacation. Your thoughts shift towards the process of planning the trip. You choose the destination, select the dates, decide on the route to take, and consider a budget that aligns with your financial situation.

"You think about the specific experiences you want to have, whether it's relaxing on a beach or hiking in the mountains. You determine the duration of the vacation and how far you are willing to travel. As you go through this process, you can already imagine yourself enjoying the trip. Your focus is solely on accomplishing that one goal.

When you eventually experience that vacation, you feel joy because of the deliberate process you went through to make it happen. You appreciate the journey as much as the destination.

"On the other hand, when you have a mere desire to go on vacation amidst a cluttered mind filled with numerous other wants, the thought lacks clarity and intentionality. Your mind is preoccupied with fulfilling other desires, and you lack a clear understanding of what exactly you want from a vacation. Even if you manage to go on vacation, without the process of setting intentions and thinking it through thoroughly, the trip can come with worries and fail to bring you joy.

"As a result, many people may later say, 'I didn't think it through' when they fail to derive pleasure from something. It may even become burdensome or lead to a negative experience after a few months."

"Desires are like a child in a candy shop, always wanting everything right away. But what happens if you actually get everything at once? You become over stimulated and end up with a stomachache."

Desires Overwhelm the Mind

I heard what Mom was saying but I still had questions. "Why is it that when we have so many desires, our minds become foggy and cluttered? Yet, when we have intentions, we can accomplish them?" I asked.

"It's all about balancing your emotions and thoughts," Mom said. "Pay close attention to your mind. Are you generating more desires that you can manage? Or are you generating intentions one at a time in an organized manner?

"Train your mind and soul. If you find yourself with a cluttered mind full of desires, free your thoughts by returning to meditation. Reconnect with your inner power, recharge yourself, and start again."

I glanced at the empty laundry basket. All the clothes were neatly folded and ready to be put back where they belonged.

No More Squinting: Trust In A Higher Power

I have been squinting for a while now, both outdoors and sometimes even indoors. The resulting wrinkles around my eyes are making me appear grumpy.

That's what happens when you live in a town where the sun shines unapologetically throughout the year. One of the things on my to-do list when my mom visited was to finally get my vision examined and order prescription sunglasses. It's a task I've been wanting to accomplish for a long time.

I dreaded going for the exam because it takes up so much time. I would end up paying as much for babysitting as I would for the glasses themselves. However, with Mom around, I made the appointment, went for the exam, and selected the glasses. Ten days later, they arrived. Finally! With prescription lenses I didn't have to squint all summer and winter.

A few days later, I found myself squinting again. I had misplaced my brand-new prescription glasses and couldn't find them anywhere. I searched high and low, left and right. I retraced my steps and called every place I had been to in the past few days. I checked the lost and found at the grocery store, the coffee shop, and the ice cream place to no avail.

I told Mom about the situation and she suggested that we say the prayer we always recite when we lose something. Together, we prayed with faith in our hearts, hoping to find the glasses. However, several more days passed, and still, the glasses remained elusive.

While we were on our way to the grocery store, I was sitting in the car with Mom. "You know what's strange?" I said. "You've always said that if we ask the universe for something, it will answer. So why hasn't the universe answered my question about where I misplaced my sunglasses? And why haven't my prayers for lost things been answered?"

Mom looked at me and replied, "Be patient, my dear. Sometimes the answers reveal themselves in unexpected ways. Search within your heart, and you will find the answer you seek."

We arrived at the grocery store parking lot, and I began to unload the stroller. After securing the kids in their seats, we made our way towards the store. As the sun shone on my baby's face, revealing her little frowning expression, I instinctively pulled down the stroller's umbrella.

To my astonishment, there were my glasses, nestled between the folds. I looked at Mom, and she looked back at me. We burst into laughter, realizing that this was the answer to our prayers. Overwhelmed with gratitude, we both started thanking God.

Mom said, "This is a sign to remind you to trust, ask, and you will always find."

Later that night, I sat with Mom and said, "Do you know what I am most thankful for today? I am really grateful for the tools that you gave me. I feel like those tools make me stronger than anything else."

"What tools are you referring to?" Mom asked.

"The prayers," I replied. "Since I was a little girl, you have always taught me how to pray. We have a prayer for everything. There's a prayer of gratitude when I buy a new dress, a prayer for protection against food poisoning when I'm skeptical about a place or certain food, a prayer for finding parking when it's difficult, and even a prayer for abundance when there's not enough.

"I have a prayer for situations where I don't want someone to see something, particularly at the airport counter when I don't want them to notice the extra pound on my luggage scale. I even have a prayer to ensure I don't burn a cake and one to keep my children safe as I send them off to school every morning."

"It's not just the prayer itself," Mom responded, "but the tools of faith and intention behind them that matter. It's about surrendering our problems and placing our trust in a higher power, believing that someone is protecting us, our children, and our endeavors. It's about having faith and completely entrusting our concerns to God. That's what true faith is all about."

As we embraced in that moment, filled with gratitude and love, I knew deep in my heart that the power of prayer would forever be our guiding light.

" "

It's not just the prayer itself, but the tools of faith and intention behind them that matter. It's about surrendering our problems and placing our trust in a higher power. That's what true faith is all about.

" "

Creating Empowering Spaces: Reprogramming Beliefs

I opened the door and was greeted by a delightful blend of aromas that transported me back to my grandmother's kitchen. The tantalizing scents of fresh bread, caramelized butter, warm honey, and a hint of cardamom filled the air. I couldn't help but feel a surge of excitement and the weariness from a sleepless night dissipating at the sight of my favorite dish awaiting me on the kitchen table. And to my delight, Mom was preparing more.

"Areka" is a beautiful ancient Arabian dish, a fusion of whole wheat bread, dates, cardamom, and honey. Mom would start by making the bread, a simple mixture of whole-wheat flour, water, and a touch of salt. She would then spread the dough like a pita bread on the pan and cook it over the stove.

Flipping the bread once, she would let it cool on the rack for a few minutes before making two or three more loaves. Next, she would bring out the food processor and add the bread, a cup of pitted dates, a tablespoon of honey, and a teaspoon of cardamom.

Blending them, the mixture transformed into a granola-like texture. Mom would serve portions in two bowls, and we would sit down to enjoy the Areka accompanied by steaming cups of coffee. With the first bite, I remarked to Mom that the aroma in the kitchen reminded me of Grandma's cooking. She looked at me with a gentle smile, cradling my baby in her arms, and said, "She is always with us."

"Let's talk about space," she went on. "Each person has a space between themselves and the outside world and events. It's within your control to create that space and to decide how you respond to those factors.

"Let me tell you a story. There were twin brothers. One was in prison, the other a successful businessman. Both were interviewed and asked the same question: 'How did you end up here?'

"The imprisoned brother replied, 'My mother was a drug addict, and my father was an alcoholic. I felt like I had no choice but to grow up lost, following the same cycle of drugs, alcoholism, and bad examples.'

"The successful twin responded, 'I had an alcoholic father and a drug addicted mother, but I made a conscious decision not to repeat their mistakes. I wanted to build a family of my own and break free from that destructive cycle.'

"These two brothers created different spaces or belief systems for themselves. One belief lifted a person up, leading to their success, while the other brought them down and led to their downfall. Our beliefs, emotions, and thoughts shape our behaviors and determine whether we succeed or fail."

"But how can we transform our beliefs, emotions, and thoughts to create behaviors that benefit us instead of working against us?" I asked.

Mom smiled. "Let's get into that. Programming your beliefs is the most crucial thing you can do for yourself. Beliefs are often formed through past experiences. You can have a conversation with your beliefs, examine how they influence your life, and make conscious choices about which beliefs to embrace.

"The energy of your soul is intricately connected to the programming of your beliefs. It effects your body, your system, and even your organs. When you have strong positive programming and beliefs, your organs function better.

"The energy of your soul can be likened to the fuel that propels the vehicle of your body. Maintaining a balanced flow of this energy nourishes your body and keeps you going. Therefore, it's important to reprogram your beliefs when you experience doubts, fear, or any negative emotions that hinder you from being your true self. These are signs that your belief system needs to be reexamined and reshaped."

"Wait, wait, wait," I interrupted. "How do we actually reprogram our beliefs? I'm certain I've asked you this question before, and I'm sure you've answered it numerous times, but please tell me again."

"You're right, my dear. Reprogramming our beliefs is a process that can be approached through meditation, pen and paper. Begin by asking yourself 'why?' and identifying the underlying emotions associated with your beliefs. Give these emotions names and jot them down on paper. Then, engage in meditation, quieting your thoughts and focusing on your breath. Only ten minutes of this practice each day can make a significant difference in your life. It will strengthen your belief system and bring about positive changes.

"Think of it as the daily cleaning and dusting you do at home to prevent the accumulation of dirt and maintain a hygienic living environment. Similarly, regularly tending to your belief system, body, and thoughts is essential for keeping them clean and harmonious. So, make it a habit to engage in this daily cleaning of your belief system."

Feeling inspired, I thanked Mom for her wisdom and guidance. With a sense of purpose, I started my day by rearranging my space.

Putting Wishes Out Into The Universe: Clearing The Fog

We had been struggling to buy a house, a longtime dream for me and my husband after living in a series of rented homes. We were at a point in our lives where we had two children and stable jobs, and we wanted to find a more permanent place to settled down. We didn't want to continue dealing with the hassle of renewing leases, communicating with landlords, and facing the uncertainty of increasing rent.

We were ready to find our perfect home, but we were not prepared to pay exorbitant amounts of money and to compete in an unreal housing market where people were paying hundreds of thousands of dollars over the asking price. We wanted to negotiate and bring the price down. The search for a home was a long and difficult road for us, with no luck at the countless open houses we attended.

Then, one day, something miraculous happened. We visited a house, recorded a video of the tour, and watched it repeatedly when we returned home. We went to bed, and the next morning, we woke up with the decision to make an offer. Surprisingly, our offer was accepted, and from that moment, everything went smoothly. Just like that, after years of searching, we became homeowners.

I asked Mom, "How did it happen? It felt like we found a lost key to a lock we'd been trying to open for so long. Sometimes we run and run and find nothing, and then suddenly something appears. What is happening there? I need to understand."

"The things you desire happen when you are in harmony with yourself and the universe," Mom said. "When you are in a state of gratefulness and meditation, when you make a wish and let it go into the universe, it comes back to you. It is the state of flow, where you are open to receiving.

"First, you have a wish. You imagine what you want happening to you and then let the wish go into the universe. Letting the wish go means not trying to control the outcome but focusing on the wish itself. Then, you must be in harmony with yourself, ready to receive what comes, and to be truly grateful for what you already have. The key to the lock has always been within you. The harmony with yourself is what unlocks what you want."

"How can we be in harmony with ourselves, and how do we know if we are not in harmony?" I asked.

"Within us, we have both clarity and fog. They are deeply connected to the things we want to see in our world. The more clarity you have, the more you can see your desired outcomes. The more fog, the more complexity and unwanted things," Mom answered.

"Okay, Mom, wait a minute. What creates clarity and fog?" I inquired.

Mom answered: "Many things create fog. Negative past experiences, negative programming or beliefs, turbulent emotions, overthinking, limited vision, or resistance can all contribute to fogginess. When you desperately want something, you may create resistance between yourself and that desired thing. When you have too many conflicting desires, manifestation becomes challenging. There are many reasons for fogginess that hinder the fulfillment of your wishes and desires. No matter what the reason for the fog, you must always go back to the source and eliminate it. Let me give you a small example of how fogginess and clarity can influence outcomes.

"Imagine you have the intention and desire to bake a cake. You start baking without knowing what kind of cake you want—chocolate, orange, or almond. You only know that you want a cake, but you have no recipe for it. As you begin baking, you realize you don't have eggs, there's only one cup of flour left, and there's no butter. You feel out of control, and the cake turns out poorly.

"However, with a clear vision, you know exactly what kind of cake you want to make. You have a recipe, gather all the ingredients, and prepare them. Everything is in front of you, and you have the time and energy to make the cake.

"With this clarity, the cake turns out well. The same concept applies to everything in life. When you have clarity and a vision of what you want to create in your reality, you gather the necessary elements, make the preparations, and create the time and energy to receive your desire. Things will manifest. On the other hand, when you have fogginess and an unclear vision, you feel lost and unprepared, and the things you desire are unlikely to appear.

"When you have a wish and realize you are in a state of fogginess, don't wait for what you want to magically appear. Take immediate action to address the fog. Go back to the reasons behind the fogginess—overthinking, negative emotions, resistance—and identify and eliminate them. Replace them with a clear vision filled with love, peace, and clarity. Then, release your wish to the universe and prepare yourself to accept and receive the answer with a heart full of gratefulness and harmony. Discovering where the fogginess lies in your vision is the most crucial step."

"So, by embracing a state of gratitude, meditation, and harmony, we open ourselves to the abundance and possibilities that the universe has to offer," I said. "We learn to let go of control and trust in the natural flow of life. As we cultivate clarity and focus on our desires, we gather the necessary ingredients, make the preparations, and create the time and energy to receive what we seek."

"Remember, clarity illuminates our path while fog obscures it," Mom replied. "Therefore, it is essential to continuously assess and address any factors that contribute to the fog. By identifying and eliminating negative past experiences, limiting beliefs, and resistance, we make room for the clear vision that leads us towards our aspirations. Do you understand now?"

I nodded my head in agreement, "Yes I do, and now I have a lot of fogginess to address."

Cleaning Out Worries: Clear Your Mind

My family faced an exciting steppingstone. We put an offer on a house and it was accepted. So, we found ourselves in the process of buying a new home. Shortly after the exciting news, I began to wonder and worry about things like packing, moving dates, and small tasks like decluttering the kitchen drawer that contained so much stuff I called it the "drawer of everything."

I worried about where to fit our belongings, when to start packing, which rooms to begin with. For a few days, I forgot the bigger idea, the great accomplishment we achieved, the amazing next stage we were about to enter as homeowners.

One morning, while having my coffee, I went to the kitchen and opened the drawer of everything. I grabbed an empty bag and started clearing and organizing. The process took less than fifteen minutes. The time I spent worrying consumed more energy and mental effort than the actual cleaning.

The lesson I learned was that I shouldn't worry about something more than the time I spend doing it. It's a lesson I keep relearning, and sometimes unlearning, only to learn it again. I made a video call to Mom on the phone.

She answered as usual, looking rested and drinking coffee, happy to see the little ones on the camera. "Mom, I have a question for you," I said.

"Ask away," she responded.

"Why do we worry so much?" I asked.

"Worries are thoughts connected to our negative beliefs," she said. "For example, the belief that everything is hard, life is hard, or that we are afraid of the future and feel insecure. Once we unpack these beliefs and understand why we think these thoughts, we realize that the outside is always a reflection of what's inside of us. When the inside is strong and connected to positive energy, like being 'plugged in,' everything outside clears out and begins to look the way we want it to. Worrying is like having a cluttered room inside you.

"In a cluttered room, there are things you might need, things you no longer need, and trash. The more worrying thoughts you have, the more your mind generates clutter. The more you worry, the more you get trapped in that cluttered room, making it harder to get out.

"Once you realize that you're standing in a cluttered room, you start thinking about clearing out some of the mess, and the easier it becomes to get out. Once you realize that you're worrying too much, you have to stop and declutter your mind from unnecessary thoughts that no longer serve you but are still hanging around. Like organizing the drawer of everything that you spent years cluttering – the cleaning out may take only a few minutes.

"Worrying will always be there. We're hardwired to worry because it's one of the survival programming traits with which we're born. Therefore, we need to create balance, my dear, a skill you need to learn over time. Controlling worry is an art that liberates you to live in love, joy, and peace.

"Now, let's talk about how to control and balance your worries. Let's start by decluttering the room of your mind. The first step is to remove the idea and belief that life is hard. We have to start thinking about how easy life is. Think about all the technology that makes our lives easier, like cooking appliances.

"Imagine how cooking was in the past compared to now. We have microwaves, air fryers, blenders, ovens, thermo mixers, gas grills, rice cookers, pressure cookers, crockpots, and more. We can cook a complete meal in minutes. Think about how, long ago, you had to hunt and gather wood to make a fire when you wanted to cook. Can you imagine how fortunate we are?

"Start with one daily activity, like turning on the faucet for water. You turn the tap and water comes out. Can you imagine how our ancestors had to collect water from natural sources? We need to appreciate the small things we use every day and compare them to how they were a hundred years ago. This practice cultivates gratitude and becomes a skill in organizing the cluttered thoughts that arise from the belief that life is difficult and hard.

"The second step is gratitude, the key to organizing your thoughts and connecting with your soul. When we are grateful, we create an energy of contentment that runs through our bodies, bringing peace and joy, much like sanitizing wipes clean and cleanse. Talk to your mind with positive thoughts and be grateful for the little things you encounter each day. Think of what made your heart sing, the things and the people that make you smile, the skills you've learned, whether they are small or big. What matters is that you think of them often and feel grateful.

"The third key step is meditation, which involves disconnecting yourself from your thoughts and worries and connecting with your inner being, your soul, and positive energy.

"The fourth step is monitoring. Now that you are aware of what worry feels like, when you start feeling worried, you will recognize the heavy sensation in your chest. Pause for a moment and acknowledge the worry. Say, 'I know what you are. I know you are the feeling of worry. You come to me with negative energy. Thank you for coming to visit, but you are no longer needed. You are welcome to leave now.'

"The fifth and final step is replacing worries with imagination. After organizing the clutter, worry will be like dusting a clean room. Replace worries with beautiful images. Imagine yourself in your new house, sipping coffee in your backyard, enjoying the views. Picture your children playing in their new rooms, you cooking in your new kitchen. Cultivating beautiful imagery adds the final touch to the cleaning process, like lighting a scented candle.

"Remember these steps, keep them in your mind, and write them down as a reference when you find yourself worrying about an event in your life. You now have the information; it's up to you how to use and apply it. Worries will go away and become manageable. Always remember that the energy goes where you focus.

The more you focus on something, the more energy you give to it. If you like something, talk about it, look at it, and give it energy then it will grow and flourish. If you don't like something that's happening in your life, try to deal with it without giving it too much focus and energy, so it doesn't become bigger and overshadow the things you like. Try to keep your worries manageable and under your control. When your mind is clear and organized, you will attract everything you want to see happening in your life.'

After this conversation, the "Decluttering the room of my mind" practice became one of my favorite activities during meditation. I always feel lighter and more organized, with a mind ready to tackle any project.

Cleaning Out Worries

"

In a cluttered room, there are things you might need, things you no longer need, and trash. The more worrying thoughts you have, the more your mind generates clutter. The more you worry, the more you get trapped in that cluttered room, making it harder to get out.

"

Saying Goodbye To The Victim: Refocusing On Gratitude

The baby had finally fallen asleep for a nap, and, feeling exhausted, I prepared my go-to lunch for those times when I don't have the energy to cook—an indulgent slice of feta cheese, nestled between halves of toasted whole wheat pita bread. I accompanied this simple sandwich with a few slices of crisp cucumber and a steaming cup of hot English breakfast tea. This meal was a cherished memory of my grandmother's quick brunch, one she enjoyed every morning.

After I finished eating, I sank down onto the rocking chair in the playroom, mismatched socks on my feet, contemplating whether to take a nap or tackle the messy house that was bothering me.

Glancing at my phone, I noticed I had a recorded message from Mom. I decided to listen and postpone the nap and cleaning the house. Mom's soothing voice instantly calmed me as she began discussing being a victim. The topic felt strangely fitting for the moment, as I indeed felt victimized with little control over my own time. Choosing between eating and sleeping seemed to be a constant struggle, and I felt like I was constantly running around.

"Often, we create the belief that we are victims," Mom said, "victims of our families, of governments, of society, and so on. These beliefs generate emotions of hate, guilt, and revenge. They make us feel that life is unfair and disconnected from our values and the source. These beliefs strip away the emotions of joy, love, and gratitude."

She explained that we could let go of this victim belief by sitting with ourselves. Taking a deep breath, we were to imagine this belief as a person, then look them in the eye, express gratitude, give them a hug, and ask them to leave. Then, we were to clean up where that person had been sitting, replacing their presence with images of strength, joy, excitement, love, and gratitude.

As I listened to the recording, I marveled at how Mom knew exactly what I needed to hear. I closed my eyes and visualized the victim figure sitting on my couch, their boots leaving muddy marks. Despite my growing anger, I thanked them and firmly told them it was time to leave. I closed the door behind them and proceeded to sanitize the areas they had touched, replacing their presence with positive imagery.

When I opened my eyes, my phone displayed a sweet text from my husband expressing his love for me. It brought a smile to my face, and somehow, I felt a surge of energy. I decided to make myself a cup of tea, play my favorite songs, and embark on cleaning the house with renewed energy.

Intentions and Beliefs: The Power to Shape Our Lives

I have always been a dreamer, someone who believes that miracles can and do happen, simply because the universe keeps proving that to me time and time again.

I've been provided this proof in various ways, across every aspect of my life. But what happens when the person we love, our spouse, or a person we hold dear, doesn't share the same belief and disagrees when we say we can achieve anything?

I asked Mom how the universe can grant my wishes if my own partner, someone who is so involved in my life, doesn't agree. How can the universe decide?

Mom responded with a single word: intentions. She explained if you believe you are the master of your life, if you believe that your outer world is a reflection of your inner self, then anything you see externally is a result of your internal beliefs.

"I want to discuss the belief that you are the architect of your life, with the ability to control what happens externally," Mom said. "Take a moment to reflect on your life, and you'll realize that everything you have is something you once dreamed of, wished for, planned, and ultimately achieved.

Every possession—the rug beneath your feet, the painting on the wall, the pots and pans in your kitchen or the significant aspects of life like home, family, spouse, children, degrees, and career—all materialized because you planned and envisioned them at some point.

If you believe that your spouse's lack of belief will hinder your accomplishments and your belief in miracles, it will. If you believe that you are capable of crafting and planning your life without relying on anyone else's beliefs, you will. If you truly desire something, the universe will conspire to make it happen.

What beliefs do you want to embrace?"

My conversation with Mom about intentions and beliefs opened my eyes to the power we hold in shaping our lives. It reminded me that the universe responds to our desires and the beliefs we hold. Whether it's the belief in miracles or the belief in our ability to plan and achieve, it is up to us to choose the beliefs that guides us.

As I move forward, I will hold on to the understanding that my partner's beliefs don't have to dictate mine. I can pursue my dreams and manifest my desires, independent of their perspective. I will embrace the belief that I am the creator of my own reality, and that the universe will conspire to bring forth what I truly want.

In the journey of life, I am filled with a renewed sense of empowerment and determination. I will continue to dream big, believe in miracles, and trust in my ability to shape my destiny. The universe has shown me repeatedly that anything is possible, and with the right intentions and beliefs, I am ready to embrace the extraordinary possibilities that lie ahead.

With gratitude for the wisdom imparted by my mom, I step into the future, confident in my ability to manifest the life I envision and nothing will stop me.

"

Take a moment to reflect on your life, and you'll realize that everything you have is something you once dreamed of, wished for, planned, and ultimately achieved.

"

Recharge and Revive: The Power of Sleep and Meditation

There was a day I remember that was just a great day. From the time I woke up, I heard the birds singing and smelled the flowers from far away. I felt happy and thankful, like I had a fresh start. I video called Mom with a big smile, and she could see my good mood right away.

"You look so happy!" she exclaimed.

"I had a wonderful, refreshing one-hour nap. It completely changed my grumpy mood, and I couldn't be happier," I said.

Mom laughed. "It's amazing how a simple nap can make you so happy. Such a small thing, but it has a big impact."

She continued, "Have you ever wondered why you feel so good after a nap? It's because sleep allows us to escape from reality. When we sleep, we give our minds a break from thinking and planning. It's a time to rest and recharge, away from the worries of the past and the future."

"Sleep not only helps our bodies and minds, but it refreshes our cells. There's another way to feel refreshed during the day – meditation. Instead of waiting for sleep, you can take short breaks, only ten minutes at a time, to relax your mind and let go of thoughts."

"If you want to feel like you've had a two-hour nap but don't have the time, try meditating for ten minutes. That's how important and beneficial meditation can be— it's like a secret superpower that can transform your mood."

"Remember to prioritize self-care and rejuvenation in your daily life. Embrace the power of sleep and the serenity of meditation to recharge your body and mind. And when life gets overwhelming, close your eyes, take a deep breath, and let the magic of rest and inner calm wash over you."

"In the journey of life, finding balance and moments of peace can truly be the greatest treasures. So go forth, sleep well, meditate often, and may your days be filled with joy, clarity, and a well-rested spirit."

There's a Gain in every Loss: Focus on the Gains

It was a serene Friday morning in spring when my husband and I embarked on the most significant wire transfer of our lives. We sent our entire life savings to purchase our dream home, a place we could call our own. I had called Mom earlier that day, sharing the bittersweet news.

"Today is the day," I told her, "We're closing on our new house. Our bank account will be emptied, but we'll gain a home in one of the priciest states in the U.S. and the world. It's hard to see our savings go, but it's worth it."

Mom responded with wisdom. "Let's talk about the gains and losses in life. We tend to focus more on what we lose, but every loss carries a gain. If we shift our focus to the gains, we can find more meaning and joy in our experiences. Dwelling on losses prevents us from fully embracing the blessings, peace, love, and gratitude that come with them."

"Always keep your attention on what you're gaining, whether it's through a transaction, a sale, or any endeavor. By focusing on the gains, you invite more blessings, love, and positive emotions into your life. Train yourself to amplify the positives and see more of what you desire."

As Mom's words settled within me, I paused and reflected on the house we had just purchased. I envisioned the memories we would create within its walls and felt an overwhelming sense of gratitude. Without a doubt, this was the best transaction we had ever made. I felt blessed to be able to afford a home in such a beautiful area and incredible state.

The excitement of becoming homeowners for the first time filled me with anticipation. I thought about my mom's words once more and realized how fortunate I was to document this moment in writing, to share with my children in the years to come.

In the end, it's not only about the loss of our savings; it's about the gains we acquire along the way. With each new chapter, we find opportunities for growth, joy, and cherished memories. Embrace the gain within the loss and appreciate the blessings that unfold in every transition of life.

Pecan Pie Conversations: The Planets of People

When she was only eighteen, Mom embarked on the greatest journey of her life – leaving her small Arabian town and venturing to the United States for the first time. In New York City she wandered through the airport. In one of the shops, she saw an unfamiliar pie. Because she was hungry, she purchased a slice without hesitation.

When Mom took that first bite, she felt as though she had tasted freedom itself. Pecan pie became the symbol of her newfound love for America, and remains her favorite dessert to this day.

Fast forwards, and I recall Mom and I sitting outside on the patio. I presented Mom with a slice of freshly baked pecan pie and a steaming cup of tea. Mom said, "Ask me anything."

I posed a question that had been on my mind for some time. "Why is it that we sometimes feel jealousy or envy when someone attains something we desire?" I asked. "Why do we compare ourselves to others and experience envy when they achieve what we want? Can't we simply be genuinely happy for one another person without those feelings?"

Mom took a moment to gather her thoughts before responding. "Imagine each person as if they were a separate planet," she began. "Every individual you encounter has their own unique weather patterns, majestic mountains, vast oceans, and even fiery volcanoes. They have their separate existence, separate from your planet. When you view others in this way, empathizing with them becomes easier. You have no knowledge of what actually transpires in their own world."

She continued, explaining the significance of this perspective. "By treating others as separate planets, you remove judgment, criticism, and assumptions about who they are or what they are going through," she said. "You acknowledge that they are entirely distinct from you. In this separation, you no longer compare yourself to others, as you realize that each person's planet is a realm you know nothing about. Instead, you offer respect for their space, decisions, and way of life. You recognize that you have no clue what lies within their planet's depths. Even the closest individuals to you, like your children and your spouse, possess their own separate planets."

As my mom enjoyed each bite of the pie, her eyes closed in pure delight, I observed her with a mix of amusement and reflection. If it weren't for her deep love for pecan pie, I would never have thought to buy it. In that moment, I imagined her planet decorated with pecan pies, a delightful and delicious realm unique to her.

Pecan Pie Conversations

"

By **treating** others
as separate planets,
you remove judgment,
criticism, and assumption.

"

Harmony in Relationships: The Okra Stew of Love

O ne lunch I enjoy making is "Bamia," an okra stew made in tomato sauce served with white basmati rice. Since I was a little girl, this dish has been, and still remains, my favorite. I often wonder, "how did a little girl have okra stew as her favorite food?"

I believe the secret lies in making vegetables tasty to children.

One afternoon, my mom was helping me make this special lunch dish. She began by dicing an onion and a couple of garlic cloves, which she added to olive oil heated in a Dutch oven. Then she added the fresh okra and sautéed it before including diced tomatoes from a can and a spoonful of tomato paste. She seasoned the mixture with salt, pepper, and freshly chopped cilantro. Finally, she poured in about 2 cups of water, covered the pot, and let it cook on low heat.

Next, she cooked about a cup and a half of rice in water, salt, and butter on medium heat. As the aroma of simmering food filled the air, we sat upstairs in the loft. Mom brought me a glass of refreshing lemonade with ice, mint, and sliced lemon. Sipping the cool drink instantly lifted my mood on that hot August day.

"So, what are we going to talk about today?" I asked.

"Relationships," she replied, explaining there are people who, by default, complain and constantly air their grievances. On the other hand, there are people whose default mode is gratitude. They always strive to make the best out of every situation. Love and passion are the guiding principles of their lives.

"What happens when these two mindsets enter into a relationship?" Mom asked rhetorically. "Regardless of the nature of the connection, the person with a mindset of love and gratitude ends up trying to please the person who constantly complains. No matter what the loving person does, the other person never finds satisfaction or happiness because they aren't geared for it. Thus, the loving person ends up suffering."

Pondering the issue, I asked Mom, "How can this issue be resolved for two people with such differing mindsets? Is there a cure?"

"The secret lies in being in harmony with yourself," she said. "No matter who your partner is, you will see what you want to see."

Intrigued, I asked if being in harmony with myself would influence the other person's energy. Mom chuckled. "No," she said. "Remember, nothing is external. It all exists within you.

You are the universe of your own being, and your harmony will reflect what you desire to see. When you are in harmony with yourself, the world will be in harmony with you."

We continued to enjoy our cold drinks as we contemplated these insights. I thanked Mom for her wisdom and guidance. She smiled warmly, her eyes reflecting pride and love. "Remember, my dear, in every relationship, be it with others or with yourself, cultivating harmony is the key," Mom said. "Nurture the love and gratitude within you, and watch as it radiates outward, touching the lives of those around you."

As we entered the kitchen, the aromas of the delicious Bamia and fragrant Basmati rice greeted us. We knew that our lunch would not only nourish our bodies but also symbolize the harmony we sought to create in our relationships and our lives.

"

You are the universe of your own being, and your harmony will reflect what you desire to see. When you are in harmony with yourself, the world will be in harmony with you.

"

Maintaining Strong Beliefs: Align with Actions

She used to be a shepherd, taking care of her sheep from sunrise to sunset every day. While out in the fields, she would often ponder the vastness of the world, the desert, and the sky. She enjoyed singing songs, eating dates, and drinking sheep's milk. Her sheep were her closest companions, following her wherever she went, joining in her songs, and running alongside her. My grandmother took great pride in her Bedouin heritage.

"I've always been proud of who my mother was and where she came from," Mom said to me one day, "even though my sister never believed our mother was a shepherdess. I loved her for who she was, but I don't think anyone truly understood her."

"She must have had a tough life, living without being understood or knowing where she truly belonged," I said.

"I saw her soul and appreciated her wisdom," Mom responded.

Curious, I asked Mom how my grandfather managed to marry my grandmother despite the obstacles. I had heard the story many times, but it always fascinated me, as I discovered new details with each telling.

Mom explained that my grandfather, a handsome man of Turkish descent with fair skin, fell in love with a Bedouin girl from the dessert. He stayed near her house for six months, deeply committed to winning her over. He asked her father for permission to marry her, but her father, bound by tribal customs, refused.

At the time, my grandfather worked as a traffic officer. He found a way to help the girl's father with a traffic-related problem, which impressed him and changed his mind. He agreed to let his daughter marry someone outside the tribe.

Reflecting on the story, I realized that a single act of kindness and understanding had a ripple effect, leading to a large and loving family. My grandparents went on to raise eight children, who then blessed them with more than fifty grandchildren and great-grandchildren.

In our conversation, Mom shared an important insight. "Sometimes our beliefs hold us back from doing great things," she said. "But when our beliefs align with our actions, we gain strength and harmony. Operating in line with our beliefs empowers us, bringing us closer to ourselves, others, and the universe. Some people use this power to persuade others to adopt their beliefs, while others focus on strengthening themselves, caring less about what others believe."

She cautioned me against adopting someone else's beliefs as my own. Instead, she encouraged me to develop strong beliefs, to stay true to them, and to let my actions reflect them. She emphasized the importance of personal power and inner strength. When we operate within our beliefs, we find harmony, and the world around us responds accordingly.

As our conversation came to an end, I shared a story about someone I met who expressed an interest in learning the Arabic language. He and a colleague started their language-learning journey. However, when an Arabic-speaking cook informed them about the various dialects and the challenges of understanding different regions, they became discouraged and gave up. Mom said that was a classic example of how adopting someone else's belief can hinder our growth.

In conclusion, Mom encouraged me to hold firm beliefs, to act in alignment with them, and to not be swayed by others' opinions. By staying connected to my inner power and remaining strong in my convictions, I would find harmony and achieve what I set out to do.

"

When our beliefs align with our actions, we gain strength and harmony. Operating in line with our beliefs empowers us, brings us closer to ourselves, others, and the universe.

"

Perfecting A Recipe: We Impact Our Relationships

One morning I woke up unable to contain my excitement. Eid is a special holiday for Muslims that celebrates the conclusion of the holy month of Ramadan. The year I'm reflecting on was one in which my mother was coming to stay with me and she made a unique request. She wanted me to cook something completely new to her. Intrigued by the challenge, I proudly told her about my latest culinary endeavor: perfecting Julia Child's beef bourguignon recipe.

So, for our Eid celebration, we decided to give the dish a try, with a side of creamy mashed potatoes. I wasted no time and got to work immediately. The recipe required time and patience, so I knew I had to start early. The day before, I bought high-quality fresh chuck meat that was ready to be sliced and cooked to perfection.

With my morning coffee in hand, I began preparing the stew. I melted a generous amount of butter in my trusty Dutch oven, relishing the rich aroma that filled the kitchen. One by one, I added the chunks of meat, watching them sizzle and brown. They looked appetizing, but I knew they still had a long way to go before being fully cooked. Carefully, I removed them from the pot, ensuring they retained their beautiful color.

In the same pot, I diced four cloves of garlic and one white onion. Adding a spoonful of butter, I sautéed them until they turned a glorious golden brown. The fragrance was intoxicating. Then, it was time to reintroduce the meat to the pot, along with a tablespoon of tomato paste, a sprinkle of salt and pepper, a handful of fresh rosemary from my garden, and a whole cup of luscious red wine. To bring it all together, I poured in some boiled water and added celery and carrots. The pot was now filled with a symphony of flavors waiting to meld and transform.

While the stew simmered on low heat, I made my way upstairs to my mother's room, carrying a steaming cup of coffee. Her face lit up with joy as I handed it to her with a plate of butter cookies.

"Thank you, dear," she exclaimed, her smile radiant. "Am I in heaven or what? Waking up to a cup of coffee and delicious treats by my side every morning is such a pleasure!"

Grinning, I replied, "Seeing you happy brings me so much joy."

In that peaceful moment, she opened up about a dream she had the previous night—one filled with memories of her in-laws and my late father. Emotions surged within her as she recalled the difficult moments and the way she had been treated in her marriage. Feelings of inadequacy, lack of support, and the constant struggle to prove herself flooded her mind. Whenever she wanted to invest in her own dreams, she felt ignored by her husband and left to fend for herself.

Mom shared the burden she carried—the weight of not being enough, of constantly feeling guilty for not meeting expectations. But then, she paused, allowing her words to sink in. With great wisdom, she conveyed a crucial lesson about relationships—one that would forever change the way I viewed myself and others.

"You see," she said, her voice filled with faith, "the thoughts we have and the way we talk to ourselves have a profound impact on our relationships. They become a mirror, reflecting back how we perceive ourselves. The way we love ourselves, treat ourselves, and engage in positive self-talk sets the tone for how others treat us."

As I listened to her words, they resonated within me. I realized that the external dynamics of our relationships are intricately linked to our internal state. If we want love, respect, and kindness from others, we must first extend those qualities to ourselves. We must become aware of our thoughts and emotions, nurturing ourselves with love and treating ourselves with dignity. It is through this self-compassion that we can truly transform our relationships.

So, I sat down with a pen and paper, ready to explore my emotions and desires. I wrote down how I wanted to be treated and how I wanted to feel in my relationships. Taking her advice to heart, I made a commitment—to treat myself with the love and respect I desired. I vowed to be gentle with myself, to silence my inner critic, and to shower myself with kindness.

I now understood that the trap of feeling stuck or taken for granted in a relationship stemmed from how I treated myself. It wasn't about ownership or possession—it was about choice and mutual respect. No one belongs to another; we are all free individuals on our unique journeys. By loving myself and treating myself with care, I could create a ripple effect, transforming the dynamics of my relationships.

If I can treat myself just like Beef Bourguignon treated me that night, it was like a loving symphony of flavors—a robust umami from the beef, a velvety richness from the red wine, a subtle sweetness from the vegetables, and a warm and earthy aroma from the herbs. The combination of these elements created a deeply satisfying and unforgettable taste experience that left me longing for more with every spoonful. It's the kind of dish that hugs the soul.

The Beef Bourguignon of relationships is about loving yourself and treating yourself with love and kindness. Now, every time I encounter someone treating me in a way I don't like, or whenever I feel taken for granted, I pause in those moments, I hear my Mom's voice echoing in my ears, reminding me, "there is no outside; there is just a reflection of how we treat ourselves from the inside.

Avatar Parenting: Embracing Parenthood with Empowerment

Mom and I went to the grocery store and stumbled upon a decadent lime cheesecake in the freezer section. Normally, I'm not a fan of frozen desserts, so I was skeptical about the taste. However, the crumbly buttery base, the fluffy middle, and the tangy lime curds on top turned looked tantalizing.

The perfectly balanced marshmallow meringue added just the right amount of sweetness to the sour lime curds. That day, I made a special trip to get this seasonal treat because one of my good friends was coming to visit with her one-year-old daughter, who was the same age as my youngest daughter.

"I think we should get this lime cheesecake. It looks delicious," I said to Mom, eyeing the dessert in the freezer.

"You're right. It does look tempting. Let's give it a try."

Excitedly, I added the cheesecake to our cart, eager to share it with my friend and her little one.

Later, when my friend arrived at our new house, I welcomed her warmly. "It's so good to see you! I've been looking forward to your visit," I said.

My three-year-old daughter, however, had a different reaction. She began throwing a tantrum and started being rude to our guests. She even started throwing things at my friend's daughter, saying she didn't want them to come over.

Horrified by my daughter's behavior, I quickly intervened, apologizing profusely. "I'm so sorry! This is completely out of character for her. Please forgive her. I don't know what's gotten into her," I exclaimed.

My friend, understandably concerned for her daughter's safety, took her in her arms and replied, "I think it's best if we leave. I can't risk my daughter getting hurt."

Feeling embarrassed and ashamed, I whispered, "I understand. I'm really sorry. I'll make sure to address this behavior."

As my friend left, she sent me a text expressing her concerns. "I don't think it's a good idea for our daughters to spend time together anymore. It's just not safe. If we meet in the future, it should be just you and your youngest," the text read.

Distressed by her message, I confided in Mom. "I feel like I've failed as a parent and a friend. I'm afraid my daughter won't have any friends and that people won't want to be around us," I said.

Mom placed a comforting hand on my shoulder and said, "every mother's job is to protect her child. Your friend needed to protect her daughter, and she did just that. Now, let's talk about you."

I looked at her, seeking guidance. "What should I do?" I asked.

"I hope one day you can delete people," Mom said, pausing to let her words sink in.

Confused, I furrowed my brow. "Delete people? What do you mean?" I asked.

"I mean removing yourself from their emotions, their troubles, and their feelings," Mom said. "Be like an avatar—a separate entity unaffected by others. You are in control of your body and thoughts. You have the power to choose what affects you."

"What's an avatar?" I questioned.

"Being an avatar means having control over your feelings, emotions, and thoughts, while also being aware of the world around you and what's happening inside yourself," Mom replied. "Here's some advice on how you can be an avatar:

- Stay Aware: Pay attention to your emotions, thoughts, and reactions. Being aware of your inner world allows you to make conscious choices in how you respond to different situations.

- Be Emotionally Detached: While empathy is important, don't let others' emotions overwhelm you. Stay true to your feelings without being consumed by the emotions of others.

- Set Boundaries: Know that it's okay to protect your inner world. Recognize what you can control and what's beyond your influence. Focus on managing your emotions instead of trying to control external factors.

- Find the Positive: In challenging situations, try to reframe negative thoughts into more positive and constructive ones. Seek solutions and opportunities for growth rather than dwelling on the negatives.

- Practice Mindfulness: Stay present and centered in each moment. Mindfulness helps you prevent past regrets or future worries from clouding your judgment and emotions.

- Develop Emotional Intelligence: Work on understanding your emotions and recognizing and empathizing with the feelings of others. This skill will help you navigate relationships with grace and understanding.

- Reflect on Your Emotions: Regularly take time for self-reflection. Identify any patterns in your emotional responses that might hold you back from personal growth and happiness.

- Cultivate Positivity: Surround yourself with positivity and engaging activities that bring joy to your life. Focus on creating moments of happiness and fulfillment.

- Be Patient: Being an avatar doesn't mean suppressing emotions; it's about processing them thoughtfully. Practice patience with yourself and others as you choose appropriate responses over impulsive reactions.

"That sounds difficult to do," I said.

Mom nodded sympathetically and responded: "It's not easy, but with practice, it becomes more natural. Embracing the avatar mindset is a journey of continuous growth and self-discovery. With this approach, you'll find strength, confidence, and happiness in navigating life's challenges. Embrace your power to choose how you respond to the world around you, and you'll lead a more fulfilling and empowered life. I believe in you, always."

Thinking aloud, I said, "But I don't want to ignore others' emotions or be unsympathetic to others."

Mom reassured me, "Of course not. It's important to acknowledge your emotions and to be empathetic. However, you can deal with people from the outside without letting them affect you or forming negative beliefs about yourself or your child based on a single experience."

I took a moment to absorb her words. "So, instead of amplifying negative behavior, I should focus on the positive feelings I want to cultivate."

"Exactly. Focus on the moments that bring you joy, the feelings you want to experience more often. They will grow and fill up your life," Mom said.

Feeling a glimmer of hope, I thanked Mom for her wisdom. "You've transformed me from an ungrateful, fearful, and frustrated mother into a calm, relieved, and empowered one. I feel grateful and blessed," I told her.

With a loving smile, Mom replied, "Every negative situation is a blessing. It appears to you as an opportunity for growth and self-reflection. Give thanks to the universe for presenting you with this event so you can use it to better yourself and guide your child's behavior."

Taking her words to heart, I embraced a sense of gratitude and released the negative emotions tied to the recent event. I closed the door to outside influences and focused on being an Avatar parent while enjoying the last slice of the lime cheesecake.

"

Embrace your power to choose how you respond to the world around you, and you'll lead a more fulfilling and empowered life.

"

Redefining Perspectives: Embracing Positivity and Letting Go

As I sat in the living room, in deep frustration and annoyance, Mom entered with a tray of mint tea and flakey baklava. Concern etched on her face, she gently asked, "Everything okay?"

Startled by her presence, I took a moment to gather my thoughts, absorbing the chaos around me. I sighed, my focus returning to the screen as I replied, "I'm tired, even though I just woke up."

"What's bothering you?" She asked gently.

Shoulders slumping, I admitted, "I'm suing my previous landlord. They unjustly kept my security deposit, and their explanations simply don't make sense. It infuriates me how often landlords get away with such things, solely driven by profit."

With a calm demeanor, Mom offered a different perspective. "Have you ever considered approaching this problem from within? Have you thought about why this event manifested in your life?" she asked. "It's a question I always ask, even though I know it can be frustrating. But it's the real question that needs to be addressed."

Defensively, I bristled at her words, asserting, "I feel that I'm a good person who doesn't deserve to be treated this way."

Nodding knowingly, Mom acknowledged my feelings. "So, you're feeling like a victim. But have you realized that the emotions of victimhood can hinder your progress?" she asked me. "They create blockages that prevent you from attracting what you truly desire. They drain your energy and overshadow the abundance of blessings already present in your life. Think about a black cloud obscuring the sun, blinding you from seeing all that you have."

Her words prompted deeper contemplation. "How can I let go of this victim mentality?" I asked.

"Visualize that victim emotion on a big screen, magnify it, and closely examine how it effects you. Then, consciously replace that feeling with positive emotions like love, peace, or joy. Recall a beautiful event or recent feeling that brought you happiness," Mom replied.

"So, whenever my mind wants to revert to that victim emotion, I'll consciously replace it with the positive emotions I've chosen," I clarified.

A smile of approval spread across Mom's face. "Exactly. By rewiring your thoughts, you'll create a new emotional landscape," she said.

Inspired, I closed my eyes, picturing the victim emotion as a person. I looked her in the eye and firmly declared, "You are not welcome here anymore. Leave." As she dissipated, I filled the void with vivid images of my upcoming vacation in Miami—feeling the warmth of the sun on my back and sinking my toes into the golden sand.

Breaking the reverie, Mom suggested, "How about we go to the grocery store? We need to pick up some milk."

With a renewed sense of hope and determination, I nodded and replied, "Sure, let's go. It's time to focus on something else and leave the victim mentality behind."

"

Visualize that victim emotion on a big screen, magnify it, and closely examine how it effects you. Then, consciously replace that feeling with positive emotions like love, peace, or joy.

"

Transforming Worries Into Peace: Take Time to Pray

I went to pick up my husband from work one day, and as soon as he got in the car, I could see the exhaustion weighing heavily on him.

Concerned, I asked, "What's wrong? Are you feeling sick?"

He shook his head. "No, it's not that. It's work. I just can't handle it anymore," my husband said.

My heart sank as I empathized with his struggle. Suddenly, my mind became a battleground for worrying thoughts, swarming like an army of ants attacking a piece of sugar.

Throughout the rest of the evening, all I could think about was our mortgage, the kids, the bills. How would I manage if my husband couldn't work anymore? What if stress took a toll on his health? The "what ifs" consumed my mind, and I couldn't escape their grip.

As I set about preparing dinner that evening, I lovingly crafted Burek, a delectable dish featuring layers of delicate filo dough enveloping seasoned ground beef and onions. Each layer was carefully brushed with an egg wash and garnished with aromatic sesame seeds before being baked to perfection in the oven. A side of crisp, fresh salad accompanied this savory delight.

While I was in the midst of cooking, Mom entered the kitchen and immediately sensed my troubled state. She extended a comforting hand and a listening ear as I poured out my concerns and fears.

After a bit, she interrupted me and said: "Listen carefully to what you're saying. Pay attention to the internal conversation you're having with yourself right now. This conversation is being led by negative energy and fueled by negative emotions.

"We often overlook the conversations we have with ourselves, but they hold immense power. These internal dialogues are filled with emotions and triggers, and if left unchecked, they tend to be overwhelmingly negative. The more negative conversations we engage in with ourselves, the more negative feelings we generate, pulling us down to the point where getting out of bed becomes a struggle."

Mom's insight helped me to acknowledge that everyone engages in self-talk on a regular basis, but rarely do people consider the impact of such internal conversations. "What can I do to change this internal dynamic?" I asked.

"The worries that creep into your mind result from the negative conversations you're having with yourself," Mom said. "Prayers, on the other hand, are conversations you have with God or a higher power. The former brings you down and doesn't lead you anywhere, while the latter has the potential to transform your circumstances and take you places."

She encouraged me to replace my worrisome, fearful, and weak thoughts with gratitude, prayers, and thoughts of the blessings in my life. Gradually, the feelings of fear and worry would be replaced with peace, gratitude, and joy. Then, I should pray for the things I wanted to see manifest in my life.

Mom emphasized that fear and worry are like gifts from the brain, urging us to pay attention, express gratitude, and redirect our focus. She advised me to thank these feelings for surfacing, forgive them for their attack on my peace of mind, and let them go.

"Forgive your body for experiencing these emotions, acknowledge the message they convey, and bid farewell to them as they depart from you. Then, pray for the outcomes you desire," Mom said.

Then, diverting the conversation to a more mundane topic, she asked, "Shall we prepare the table?"

"Dinner is ready," I said.

That evening, we indulged in the Burek, savoring each bite of its crispy layers and the perfectly seasoned ground beef. The accompanying salad was the ideal companion to the dish, their flavors working in harmony, like the best of partners in a dance. For a moment, the Burek had the power to make me forget my worries, allowing me to be fully present and relish every delightful mouthful.

Later that night, as I lay my head on the pillow, I gazed out of the window at the night sky. I began to pray, pouring my hopes and dreams into each word, until a sense of peace washed over me, lulling me into a peaceful sleep.

Ask The Question: Receive The Answer

A few days after moving into our new house, we had the chance to meet our next-door neighbors. They were a lovely couple with a baby girl. After introducing ourselves and engaging in small talk, my family and I headed out to the beach.

As we were driving, I turned to my husband and said, "I really like our new neighbors. They seem like nice people, and their baby girl is adorable."

He nodded and replied, "I agree."

Then, a thought crossed my mind, and I paused before asking, "I can't help but wonder, what do they do for a living?" I hesitated to ask because in our culture, it can be considered rude to inquire about someone's occupation right after meeting them.

A few days later, I went to the grocery store, which happened to be located next to a furniture shop. Deciding to make the most of the proximity, I parked my car between the two establishments, planning to visit both in one go. Although I frequented the grocery store often, it was the first time I had parked in that particular spot.

As I was walking, I noticed a tailor shop nestled between the grocery store and the furniture shop. Intrigued, I stopped and admired the dresses and suits on display. Then, my eyes fell upon a mug with an image of a man holding his baby girl. It read, "Daddy and Me." The image caught my attention, and something about the faces of the father and baby seemed familiar. Continuing on my way to the grocery store, I couldn't shake off the feeling.

On my return to the car, I passed by the tailor shop once again, and this time I recognized the familiar faces from the mug. It was indeed our new neighbor, waving at me.

Excitedly, that evening, my mom prepared an afternoon dessert dish called Kunafa. We gathered our ingredients and equipment. It was a cherished traditional dish in our family, and we couldn't wait to create this treat together.

First, we had already bought the Kunafa dough, which was a fine, shredded pastry that would form the base of the dessert. As we worked, the kitchen filled with the warm aroma of butter as we layered the pastry into a baking dish, creating a golden, crispy foundation.

Next came the sweet and fragrant filling, a combination of finely chopped nuts, often including pistachios and walnuts, mixed with a touch of sugar and aromatic spices. The combination of textures and flavors was something to look forward to.

Once the filling was generously spread over the pastry layer, we added another layer of Kunafa dough on top. The dish was ready to be baked.

As it baked, the kitchen was suffused with the scent of buttery pastry and toasted nuts. The Kunafa slowly turned a beautiful shade of golden brown, and we couldn't wait to drizzle it with a fragrant sugar syrup, allowing it to soak up the sweetness.

When the Kunafa was finally ready, we shared the warm, crispy dessert, garnished with a sprinkle of more chopped nuts. It was a moment of pure joy, not just in savoring the delightful taste but in the bonds we strengthened as we created this cherished dessert together.

As we sat down to eat, I shared the discovery of what I had seen today. She responded, "You know, every question you ask the universe will be answered. The answers will reveal themselves to you. There is a universe inside you, where all your questions and their answers reside. Everyone has this power; can you believe it?"

I nodded in agreement, realizing that I often had questions about people's occupations and a curiosity to understand how they made their living and how much they earned.

"And once you ask those questions, you will find the answers," Mom said. "They are within you."

I looked up, feeling a sense of empowerment and confidence, knowing that I held all the answers to my questions.

"

There is a universe inside you, where all your questions and their answers reside.

"

The Power of Imagination and Intention: All Credit Goes to a Higher Power

Mom and I decided to create a mouthwatering Middle Eastern dish known as "Warag Onab," meaning grape leaves. This delightful delicacy consists of seasoned rice and ground beef, individually wrapped in grape leaves and cooked in a savory tomato sauce.

It's a symphony of flavors, with a hint of sourness from the tangy lemons and a secret ingredient I learned from Mom: pomegranate syrup. I adore this dish, but I rarely find the time or inclination to painstakingly wrap each grape leaf. Fortunately, Mom has a special technique that makes the process effortless.

Mom began gathering the ingredients. She measured a cup of short-grain rice, rinsed it, and placed it in a bowl. Next, she finely chopped an onion and measured a cup each of fresh cilantro and dill, adding them to the rice along with a diced tomato.

Seasoning the mixture with salt, pepper, the juice of one lemon, and half a cup of olive oil, she gave it a thorough mix. Mom then retrieved the preserved grape leaves from the Middle Eastern store, effortlessly unwrapping them one by one while enjoying the background music of the one and only Umm Kulthum. Her songs, are slow-paced with a mathematically repetitive structure that features deep, resonant notes that transition to soaring highs. Her voice carries a certain warmth and richness that captivates, conveying a profound depth of emotion.

Before we knew it, a stack of perfectly wrapped grape leaves awaited us. Mom took a pot and coated the bottom with olive oil, layered thinly sliced onions and potatoes, and carefully arranged the wrapped leaves. Pouring in diced tomatoes, a pinch of salt, and about a quarter of a cup of pomegranate syrup, she covered the pot and set it on low heat.

"Do you know the secret to cooking?" she asked.

"Love," I answered.

"Indeed," Mom smiled, "love is essential, but there's more. Imagination and intention play a significant role."

She explained that even before we step into the kitchen or begin any task, we must imagine what we want to create—the final result, the flavors, and the presentation. Imagination acts as the initial spark, while intention guides our actions. It's as if imagination and intention are tiny fairies, guiding our hands through the process.

"I'm merely the vessel," Mom said. "There is a higher power at play, utilizing our hands to bring about the desired outcome. By relieving ourselves of the burden and understanding that we are co-creators, we open ourselves to the wondrous possibilities."

Mom shared her thoughts on the majestic pyramids of Egypt, expressing awe at their construction. "These inspiring wonders were built by people like us, without modern technology," she said. "How could they withstand the test of time? The answer lies in the power of intention and imagination. One brick at a time, with the aid of a higher power, they manifested."

The key lesson, Mom emphasized, is to not carry the weight of the world solely on our shoulders. Instead, we should see ourselves as instruments of the higher power, working hand in hand. By surrendering to the greater force, we can achieve remarkable feats, both big and small.

From cooking a meal to writing a book or constructing a bridge, it's all about letting go and trusting in the collaboration between our imagination, intention, and the higher power. In Arabic, we say, "Asta'enei be Allah," which means "Seek help from God and take action."

Mom added that there's also a saying in Arabic that encourages us to seek God's assistance even for something as small and readily available as salt. "No task is too trivial to seek divine guidance," she noted.

As 45 minutes ticked by, the tantalizing aroma of the grape leaf dish permeated the air. Mom exclaimed, "Let's eat!" Plating a portion for me, I eagerly took the first bite with my favorite fork. The taste was nothing short of extraordinary, and it felt as if our home had never before been full of such enticing flavors.

With a mouthful of deliciousness, I looked at Mom in amazement and exclaimed, "Wow, Mom, this is one of the best things I've ever tasted! How did you make it so incredibly delicious?"

Mom, pointing her finger skyward, replied with a smile, "Honestly, I have no idea. All credit goes to a higher power."

Dreams Do Come True: Prepare Yourself

I went to Mom's room to say goodnight and found her sitting on the bed, immersed in a prayer book she'd owned for as long as I could remember. Its pages were worn out, almost falling apart from years of use.

When I sat beside her, Mom said, "Do you know what I just realized? Dreams always come true."

"I believe they do come true, sooner or later," I replied.

"Have you ever had a dream for a very long time, and when it finally came true, you felt thrilled at first, but then you looked around and thought, 'Is that it? Is this how I am supposed to feel?'" Mom asked.

I nodded, understanding the sentiment. Mom went on: "Some people feel depressed or disappointed after their dreams come true because they expected to feel fantastic and grateful, but in reality, they didn't.

"They wonder what's wrong with them, like someone who wanted a certain job and, upon finally getting it, realizes they are not enjoying the work as much as they thought.

"When we attract something in life, we also attract the accompanying feelings. Imagine someone feeling down and depressed because they hate their current job. They desperately want to find another job that brings them happiness. Even when that new job becomes a reality, however, their feelings of depression and dissatisfaction tag along. That's why they continue to feel the same, even in a changed situation."

"How can we ensure we experience the joy and happiness we desire when our dreams come true?" I asked.

"It all comes down to the preparation," Mom responded. "Before attracting what you want, start by preparing the emotional ground. Cleanse and declutter any unwanted emotions."

She grabbed a pen and paper, instructing me to do the same. "Write down how that dream job would make you feel. Will it bring gratitude, joy, and excitement?" she said. "Will you feel loved, accomplished, and appreciated? Visualize those feelings, even in your current situation or job, and find the beauty and gratitude within it.

"By aligning your emotions with love, joy, and gratitude before your dreams manifest, you'll carry those feelings into your new reality," Mom continued. "That way, when you finally achieve what you desire, you'll experience the happiness and fulfillment you sought."

We sat together gazing out her window. "Look at the moon," Mom said, her voice filled with wonder.

"It's magnificent tonight," I replied.

Mom nodded in agreement. In that moment, we understood that the beauty of life lies not only in achieving our dreams but also in appreciating the little wonders that surround us.

"

Before attracting what you want, start by preparing the emotional ground. Cleanse and declutter any unwanted emotions.

"

Letting Go of Fears: Enjoying the Moussaka

Mom asked, "What's for dinner?" I didn't have anything planned, but I was hoping Mom could direct me in a recipe if I told her what ingredients I had on hand. I replied, "We have an eggplant."

"Then let's make Moussaka," Mom said.

In Arabic, Moussaka means "cold," and refers to a dish that can be eaten either cold or warm. It always tastes even better the next day. Moussaka consists of layers of eggplant, onion, and potato casserole with ground beef and tomato sauce.

Every time I eat Moussaka, it feels like a comforting hug. Like a bride on her wedding day, dressed in her finest gown and glowing, I always picture eggplant at its best in Moussaka – there's no better way for an eggplant to shine.

Mom began by slicing an onion, a big potato, and an eggplant. She also defrosted a cup of ground beef. She cooked the meat with onions and olive oil, then added a couple cloves of garlic and a can of tomato sauce, along with some salt and pepper. She sprinkled in some chopped cilantro and let it cook on low heat for about 10 minutes.

Next, she deep-fried the slices of potato and eggplant until they turned brown and crispy. In an oven-safe pan, she layered the slices. She poured the tomato and beef sauce on top, added more cilantro, and drizzled on two tablespoons of pomegranate molasses. She put the pan in the oven at 400 degrees and let it bake for about fifteen minutes until it browned. Meanwhile, I prepared basmati rice as a side dish.

We sat at the table, and Mom shared a story. "I remember once when I was a teenager, I went to visit my brother in London, where he was studying," she said. "My mother, my sister, and I made the trip. I still remember the shame and fear that rushed through my body when my mother chose to pray the Islamic prayer under a tree on campus."

Mom feared the reaction of the people around them, terrified of any potential negative response. Would someone say something? Giving her mother looks? Laugh during the prayer?

She reflected on the situations in which many people find themselves—a mother on a plane with a crying baby or a man introducing his girlfriend to his parents for the first time. Even presenting an idea at work to a tough audience could elicit fears of hurtful comments or reactions.

"These hidden fears weaken us in different ways," Mom said. "They prevent us from speaking up or standing up for ourselves, and they create barriers to achieving our goals and desires. They keep us confined within our comfort zones."

"How do we deal with these fears of what others think of us or what they might say?" I asked.

"Simply recognizing and acknowledging our emotions is enough," Mom responded. "We need to understand what we're feeling in the moment, be present, and welcome those feelings. Then, we can let them go."

"But how do I let them go?" I asked.

"By acknowledging them, they will naturally dissipate on their own," Mom said.

We set up the table outside and enjoyed every bite of our meal. The flavors danced on our palates, creating a sense of warmth and contentment. The sunset painted the sky in pink and purple and in that moment, I realized that the fear of others' judgment and the weight of societal expectations could be released, like the worries that vanished into the evening sky. We embraced the joy of being present, enjoying the simple pleasures of delicious food and breathtaking sunsets. With each passing moment, we let go of those little fears that once held us back.

"

We need to understand
what we're feeling in the
moment, be present, and
welcome those feelings.
Then, we can let them go.

"

The Reflection of the Mind: Shaping Your Experiences

I woke up and the baby was crying. I ate breakfast, but the baby was still crying. I had my coffee, brushed my teeth, vacuumed the floors, picked up the toys, washed the dishes, watered the plants, and the baby was still crying.

At some point, desperation overwhelmed me. I felt trapped alone in a space with my ears taped to a horn. Someone kept honking the horn making my ears and heart ache. I couldn't think straight or feel my emotions. I was numbed by the pain, stuck with no solution.

I turned to my mother. "Mom, I'm tired of the baby constantly crying and shouting in my ears," I said with exasperation.

"Do you know that the instant you leave the house, the baby stops crying?" Mom replied.

"But even when I'm out, it seems like I hear babies crying all the time," I said.

"Haven't you realized that it's your thoughts crying and shouting in your head?" Mom asked.

Then it hit me. She was right. My thoughts were the horn. They were screaming.

"Try to wipe the spot on your face, not the one on the mirror this time," Mom said. "Everything, and I mean everything, is a reflection of what's in your mind. You can leave the baby here with me and go somewhere else, but don't take your thoughts with you because the crying sound will follow you no matter where you go. Let's fix this from the inside now."

"How?" I asked, eager to know the way to make to the crying stop following me around.

"Meditation," Mom said. "Slow down your thoughts until they come to a complete stop."

"That's easier said than done," I said.

"Gratitude is the secret," Mom responded. "It's the only way to slow down your negative thinking and silence the crying baby in your head. God has given us everything—land, plants, the sun, and the moon. When God gives us money, we think about how to invest it, spend it, save it, pay less taxes, and so on.

"When we don't have money, we think about how to get it, how to pay bills, and so forth. The default human brain is always in a complaining state, bringing negative feelings and emotions. The only way to discipline your mind is through gratitude and positive ideas and thoughts.

"Each morning, when you wake up, you feel angry and upset until you have that first cup of coffee in your hand. Then, you start to feel better. The brain is accustomed to start complaining from the time you open your eyes in the morning. If you don't discipline it, the brain will continue its negative patterns. Tell your brain to stop, say you're grateful for the coffee, appreciate how the aroma fills the air. Contain and discipline your brain so that it will provide you with more positive thoughts and experiences.

"That's why the prayers we say when we first open our eyes in the morning are reminders to be grateful. 'Thank you, God, for giving us another day to wake up and be alive.' Train yourself to say a prayer upon waking and initiate a change from your default thoughts toward gratitude."

"Okay, Mom. Take the baby now," I said. "I need get this honking horn in my head turned off."

With a renewed sense of clarity and a newfound understanding of the power of gratitude, I left my mom's place determined to make a change. As I walked away, I noticed the beauty in the simplest things around me—the chirping of birds, the gentle breeze against my skin, and the vibrant colors of flowers in full bloom.

I embarked on a journey of self-discovery, armed with the knowledge that the key to quieting the chaos within was through gratitude. Each morning, I woke up and whispered a prayer of thanks for the gift of a new day. I savored my morning coffee, allowing its warmth to awaken my senses and fill me with appreciation. I practiced mindfulness and meditation, gradually slowing down my thoughts and embracing the present moment.

In time, the once-persistent cries in my head transformed into a symphony of gratitude and positivity. I realized that the external circumstances might remain the same, but my internal perspective had shifted. I had learned to find joy in the midst of challenges and to see the blessings that surrounded me.

As I reflect on that transformative conversation with Mom, I'm grateful for her wisdom and guidance. She showed me that the power to change our reality lies within our minds. By cultivating a mindset of gratitude, we can break free from the chains of negativity and embrace a more peaceful and fulfilling existence.

And so, armed with gratitude as my morning prayer, I walked forward, ready to face whatever life had in store, knowing that the reflection of my mind would shape my experiences and lead me to a place of happiness and contentment.

Embracing the Gifts Within: Nurturing Negative Emotions

As we drove to the grocery store that my mom adored—a big box store where the aisles seemed to last forever—she spoke passionately about its abundance and how it symbolized America for her.

Although she enjoyed finding quality clothes at great deals, she never ventured near the food section. "It's just too much food," she would say. "It'll go bad, or you'll get bored of it before you even open it. You already feel full just looking at it." So, whenever we visited, we headed straight to the section with the quality sweatshirts she liked to buy.

I suggested that we go alone to the store, leaving the kids with my husband, so we could take our time and indulge in some browsing. There was something satisfying and curiosity-nurturing about exploring each item and aisle, feeding our senses with the visual abundance.

As we drove to the store together, Mom suddenly said, "Negative emotions are like gifts." Intrigued, I asked her to elaborate. She explained that negative emotions were messages our bodies sends us, trying to convey something important.

"Let's say you wake up feeling angry," she said. "That anger and rage flow through your veins, and if you ignore those feelings, they will manifest in events. You'll encounter people who are angry with you—a boss getting upset, witnessing arguments, or even a car accident with people screaming at each other. If you ignore the anger, it will manifest in your body as pain. You might develop a headache, toothache, or back pain. The more you ignore or try to numb the pain with temporary relief like painkillers, the stronger it may become, this time in the form of diseases."

Her words struck me. I realized how our bodies suffer to deliver messages to us, only to be ignored.

"Once you experience negative emotions," she said, "whether it's anger, sadness, or worry, and you begin to see the cycle of negative events unfolding, stop right there. Embrace and welcome those negative emotions, receiving them with gratitude for surfacing. Write them down and ask them questions—where they came from, why they are here, and what message they bring. Write down the answers. Ask and write, even if it may seem silly, for the sake of your mental health.

"After you have all the answers," she continued, "meditate and bid farewell to these emotions. Thank them for appearing and let them know you've received their message. Replace these emotions with gratitude and love. Thank them and say goodbye, then move on. By acknowledging and facing them head-on, they will stop right there.

"These are healthy habits," she concluded. "I want you to always practice them when you receive the gift of negative emotions. Never ignore those feelings, always accept and receive them, and then unpack and explore them. Thank them and bid them farewell."

As we arrived at the store's parking lot, I expressed my appreciation for the ample parking spaces. Mom responded with a smile, "They represent what awaits inside the store." We shared a laugh, ready to embark on our shopping adventure.

"

Negative emotions
are like gifts, they are
messages that our bodies
sends us, trying to convey
something important.

"

The Matrix of Societies: You Have Options

After they enjoyed our cherished family recipe of oats tomato soup for lunch, the kids played happily in the backyard. Even as contentment filled the air, Mom asked, "What shall we make for dinner?"

"How about spaghetti?" I suggested.

And so, the plan was set in motion to create two delectable sauces: one with mushroom and cream, the other with tomatoes.

With the water boiling and the spaghetti prepared to perfection, I carefully orchestrated the two flavors in separate pans. Slicing onions, sautéing garlic, and adding the finest ingredients, I crafted a creamy mushroom sauce in one pan and a rich tomato sauce in the other.

As the sauces simmered, I drained the spaghetti and divided it between the pans, garnishing both with freshly chopped parsley and grated parmesan cheese. The table was set, and despite having already eaten, the kids eagerly joined us once again.

With the first bite, Mom expressed her delight, exclaiming, "It tastes amazing!" Amidst the harmonious sounds of laughter and shared moments, our dinner became more than a meal—it became a catalyst for an enlightening conversation.

"Do you know," Mom said, "that every society lives within something called a matrix? These matrixes are constructed for people to follow, for economies to thrive, and for governments to exert control. They dictate when schools start, when weekends occur, and when holidays are scheduled. People plan their lives around these matrixes, but only a few dare to step outside their confines."

"But," I interjected, "isn't it impossible not to follow such constructs?"

Mom smiled. "Our family has never adhered to these matrixes," she said. "We planned our vacations in the middle of the school year and went grocery shopping late at night when we felt wide awake. We challenged the conventional notion of time. Remember our driver who used to call our house 'unorganized?' Yes, routine is important, especially for kids and families in society. However, it's vital to follow routines with awareness, always conscious of how a routine benefits your family."

"I understand," I said. "Those who can defy the matrix must have options."

With a triumphant gleam in her eyes, Mom exclaimed, "Exactly! When you have options and create more of them for yourself, you're aware of possibilities, and you become stronger and happier. If a job, a city, or even a country isn't working for you, there are countless alternatives out there. You have the power to go anywhere in the world. That's the mindset I want you to adopt.

"By doing so, you'll pave the path to freedom. Some people believe they can only do one job or live in one place, but they are unknowingly imposing limitations upon themselves, blindly following a predetermined path due to their inability to see the array of options available."

As we finished the last bites of our spaghetti, a deep sense of fulfillment washed over us. It was more than a satisfying meal; it was a moment of realization, a reminder to always question and evaluate, to seek alternatives and embrace the power of choice.

With gratitude in our hearts and a newfound understanding, we cleared the table, knowing that this conversation had left an indelible mark on our journey through the matrix of societies.

The Matrix of Societies

"

When you have options and create more of them for yourself, you're aware of possibilities, and you become stronger and happier. If a job, a city, or even a country isn't working for you, there are are countless alternatives out there. You have the power to go anywhere in the world. That's the mindset I want you to adopt.

"

Live In The Moment: Remember The Memories

While the dryer was tending to the laundry, I glanced in the mirror and thought, "I really need a haircut." My unruly hair seemed to be going in all directions. I grabbed my phone and started searching for a haircut appointment at the salon nearest to my house.

Mom, who was nearby, remarked, "Oh, I miss my hairdresser. He's such a talented man. Have I ever told you about the story of my hairdresser?" I replied, "No, you haven't."

She began, "I have a talented hairdresser in Egypt. He, his wife, and daughter run the salon together, each having a specific role. They manage it beautifully. Every time I visit his salon, he talks about his time living in Lebanon. He speaks of it as if he's still there. I thought he still had the salon he often mentioned in

Lebanon, describing the celebrities who were his clients and the salon's appearance, the streets of Lebanon, and the country's beauty. It was always delightful to hear about his experiences, and I loved how his eyes would light up when he spoke of his salon in Lebanon."

"But then," she continued, "I asked the hairdresser if he still had his salon there. He said no, that was about 20 years ago. I was shocked by how vividly he recalled the details of something that happened two decades ago."

"So I asked him right away: 'Tell me about your salon here in Egypt. Who are your celebrity clients here? How's this country? Who do you know in this street?' It was then that he started to live in the moment, discussing his current salon and his recent clients. He was transported back to the present. Now, whenever I see him, I inquire about how his current salon is doing and who his interesting customers have been recently. Over time, I realized that he's often living in the moment, updating his salon, hanging up more current photos on the walls, and immersing himself in the 'now.'"

I interjected, "But I think everyone has beautiful memories they like to talk about." Mom responded, "Well, there's a difference between recalling a memory and living in the memory. When you live in the past memory, you miss the creation of new memories and the joy of current events. You lose the magic of the present moment. Life is full of experiences, so why cling to just one when there are so many others to enjoy and carry with you?"

Mom continued, "The more experiences you go through, the more you can fully appreciate life. Remember the good memories without dwelling in them. Create new ones by living in the now and appreciating every step of your journey. That's my advice to you." We then started folding the laundry.

The Weight of Responsibility: We Were Made for Joy

"Mom," I said, "how about we go for ice cream after dinner?"

"That's a great idea!" Mom responded, excited.

I cooked light food for our supper in anticipation of the coming treat. I roasted vegetables with garlic, rosemary, and olive oil. With asparagus, cauliflower, and carrots on hand, I heated drizzled olive oil in a pan, added garlic, and watched the contents brown before introducing the vibrant vegetables. Over medium heat, I roasted them, adding rosemary from the garden, along with a sprinkle of sea salt and black pepper.

Alongside the roasted veggies, I served air-fried potato patties, layering the vegetables delicately upon them. To enhance the flavors, I generously sprinkled shredded parmesan over each plate. As we enjoyed our meal, satisfied and content, we soon found ourselves strolling toward the ice cream shop.

As we entered, the scent of freshly churned ice cream filled the air. Mom indulged in a delightful banana split, with three scoops of walnut caramel, dark chocolate, and coffee, all topped with a cascading blend of hot caramel sauce and chocolate fudge. With the first spoonful, she turned to me and said, "You know, your problem is that you worry too much."

Perplexed, I responded, "How can I not worry? I have the responsibility of caring for the kids—feeding them, getting them to school, keeping them safe."

Gently, she leaned closer and shared her wisdom, saying, "Do you truly believe that you alone keep them alive? Are you the one who created them?"

I hesitated before admitting, "No, but even thought it may be arrogant of me, I do believe I am responsible for everything in their world."

Her eyes softened. "That burden is too heavy for you to carry," she said. "You are merely a vessel, chosen to carry and nurture these children. Every child comes into this world with their own protection, their own guardian. Think of it as you being the hands through which a higher power cares for them.

"Whenever you embark on something or strive to create, seek help from the divine. Trust that the power to succeed will be bestowed upon you, and before you know it, you will have fulfilled your part. Connect with your inner self, tap into the source of your strength. When life becomes overwhelming, and things aren't falling into place, reconnect and take a moment to close your eyes, breathe deeply, and ask for the higher power to flow through you. Soon, you'll witness the manifestation of your desires. Life is not meant to be shouldered alone."

As I enjoyed my nutty coffee ice cream, her words filled me with a surge of happiness. This, I realized, is what life is truly about—finding joy and being present in the simple pleasures. With gratitude in my heart, I embraced the present moment, understanding that joy is the purpose for which we are all created.

"

When life becomes **overwhelming**, and things aren't falling into place, reconnect and take a moment and ask for the higher power to flow through you.

"

Embracing Emotional Resilience: Navigating Separation

As we drove home from our shopping excursion, a tinge of sadness lingered in the air. The realization sank in that Mom's departure overseas was drawing near. The weight of her absence started to settle on my shoulders, and I felt a sense of unease.

With a heavy heart, I turned to Mom and mustered the courage to broach the topic that had been weighing on my mind. "Mom, I know you'll be leaving in a few days, and I feel unprepared for you to go," I said.

Mom, with her comforting smile, understood my mixed emotions. "How would you prepare yourself?" she gently asked, recognizing the vulnerability in my voice.

"I don't know," I admitted.

A soft chuckle escaped her lips as she reflected on the bond we shared. "As if I never weaned you," she said, playfully acknowledging the enduring connection we had nurtured over the years.

While the drive continued, the conversation took an introspective turn. I told Mom about a concern that had been shared with me by a friend. Her daughter, a bright first-grader, had been struggling with separation anxiety during school drop-offs.

The thought lingered in my mind, and I couldn't help but wonder: Until what age do these emotions persist in children? That's when it hit me. Despite the passage of time, I, too, harbored a lingering sense of separation anxiety from my mother.

Recognizing the weight of my emotions, I confided in Mom, seeking solace and guidance. She listened attentively. "I'm glad you used the term 'prepare myself' rather than 'protect myself,'" she remarked, noting the subtle distinction that would shape our conversation.

Intrigued, I probed further, eager to understand the difference. Mom patiently explained, "When you protect your emotions, the result is often negative. It's crucial to acknowledge and feel your emotions, to understand why they arise. But if you shield yourself from these emotions, that's rooted in fear. And any form of protection fueled by fear is bound to have adverse effects."

Her words challenged the notion of protecting oneself from emotional upheaval. Mom continued, offering examples that illustrated her point. Shielding our children from potential harm due to fear of injury in a particular sport, safeguarding our hearts from love to avoid heartbreak, or even protecting ourselves from failure by never venturing into new opportunities—all these forms of protection stem from fear and limit our ability to fully experience life's emotional spectrum.

"Do not protect anything out of fear," she advised earnestly. "Allow yourself to feel all your emotions, for protection rooted in fear only breeds negativity."

Her wisdom was apparent as she addressed my concerns about protecting my children from illness through vaccinations. With a gentle smile, she reassured me, "That's different, my dear. Protection driven by fear is distinct from being proactive, which is both wise and necessary. Instead of protecting out of fear, be proactive."

Being proactive means finding alternatives to fear-based protection. For instance, rather than preventing our children from playing a certain sport out of fear of injury, we can proactively choose a sport that aligns with their needs and age.

Similarly, instead of shielding our emotions from the pain of separation, she encouraged me to explore proactive strategies. Filling my schedule to distract myself from her impending departure wouldn't offer genuine protection—it would merely serve as a temporary escape. Being proactive, on the other hand, involved learning how to uplift oneself during moments of sadness and disconnection.

Mom imparted practical ways to be proactive in protecting our emotional well-being. She suggested identifying activities or practices that uplifted the spirit, such as listening to a favorite song that ignited joy, engaging in a prayer that fostered a positive sense of connection with the soul, watching a meditation video that offered solace, or simply embracing moments of silence that restored inner calm. These proactive measures, she assured me, would help me navigate the emotional landscape with resilience and strength.

Grateful for her insight, I expressed my appreciation for reminding me of these valuable lessons. With her comforting reassurance, Mom emphasized, "Don't worry, my dear. We are resilient beings, and physical distance does not diminish our mental connection. Our emotional bond surpasses the limitations of physical proximity."

Her words echoed in my mind, filling me with a newfound confidence. "You're right," I admitted, acknowledging the strength within me. "We will overcome this challenge together."

As the car journey continued, I inhaled deeply, appreciating the fresh air, and I realized that the power to lift myself resided within. Mom lovingly advised against depending on her as a mediator for connection or happiness. She reminded me that I didn't need anyone else—I was a universe unto myself. A profound sense of understanding washed over me as I absorbed her words.

Intricacies of Fear: Replacing with Gratitude

As we loaded the suitcases into the car, my heart felt heavy. As usual, Mom, wore a warm smile. Clad in a pink sweater, she was ready to embark on her journey home. The three months she spent with us had flown by, and now it was time to say goodbye. We decided to leave early to enjoy a final pizza dinner before heading to the airport.

During the car ride, I couldn't help but express my thoughts to Mom. "Why is it that fear sometimes enters our hearts?" I asked. "I find myself becoming fearful even in the face of small or ordinary things. Worst-case scenarios often creep into my thoughts, weakening me and enveloping me in fear."

"Fear emerges when you are in a low vibration, when you are out of harmony with yourself, when you feel disconnected," she said.

Intrigued, I asked her how I could reconnect.

"Start with gratitude," Mom said. "Focus on the things you truly love and are grateful for in your life. It's not about thinking of what you should be grateful for; it's about acknowledging and appreciating the things that genuinely bring you joy."

I closed my eyes, grateful that my husband was the one behind the wheel. The thought of the box of cheese that my husband's uncle has sent us from his cheese factory brought immense gratitude to my heart. I envisioned the recipes I will create with the fresh, creamy gorgonzola, the nutty aged parmesan, and the melty mozzarella that will elevate my homemade pizzas to new heights. A sense of happiness washed over me.

My mother noticed the smile on my face. "Are you still scared?" she asked.

I responded, "Scared? Of what? I have nothing to fear. I'm grateful for the time we've spent together and for the knowledge and tools you have shared with me."

As we arrived at the airport, I kissed Mom goodbye, my heart overflowing with gratitude and confidence in the tools she had bestowed upon me. It felt as if she had stocked my fridge and pantry with a wide array of ingredients and equipped my kitchen with every tool imaginable.

I felt an excitement building within me, an eagerness to explore and master various situations armed with these resources. Above all, I carried the assurance that I had someone to turn to whenever I needed support.

Until our paths crossed again and we forged more precious memories together, I bid Mom farewell, cherishing the bond we shared.

www.ingramcontent.com/pod-product-compliance
Lightning Source LLC
Chambersburg PA
CBHW071157130626
46553CB00004B/1698